T H

SMALL
GROUP

52 ways to help you
and your small group grow

Dave Earley • Rod Dempsey

Published by TOUCH® Publications, Inc.
P.O. BOX 7847
Houston, Texas 77270 USA
(800) 735-5865 • Fax (713) 896-1874
www.touchusa.org

Cover and illustrations by Mark Neubauer

International Standard Book Number: 0-9788779-2-6

Additional copies of this book can be purchased at a
substantial savings off the retail price by buying directly
from the publisher. Quantity discounts are also available.
Details can be found on our web site or by calling our
toll free number listed above.

Table of Contents

Introduction

We had just finished a Saturday morning training seminar for new small group leaders in a large church. Afterward, Dan and his wife, Kim, thanked us for coming to their church. They were excited about their future, but we could tell they were apprehensive about launching out into small group leadership.

Then Kim looked at us intently. With a big smile she asked, "Which one of you will go home with us until we get this right?" Of course, we couldn't go home with them and we can't go home with you either—but we can help you!

Why we wrote this book

Small group leadership is one of the hardest, yet most fulfilling challenges one can accept. We also collaborated on this book for three other reasons.

Reason #1 - Small group leadership demands immense patience and perseverance. It is extremely difficult to work for a harvest that seems slow in coming. At times it feels like the enemy is fighting you every step of the way, doesn't it? This book provides encouragement in strong doses.

Reason #2 - After you lead a group for a few years, there may be a temptation to rely on your own experience, knowledge, and insight. By working through this pocket book a few pages a day during your devotional time, it will serve as a reminder that the spiritual life of the group flows from the giver of life, Jesus Christ.

Reason #3 - It's common for leaders to fall into a routine or a rut. You may find yourself doing what you have always done with the same old results. Is your group stagnant or meetings monotonous? In this book, you'll find fresh ideas, practical suggestions, and a new perspective.

Why so many short chapters?

Learning to lead a healthy, growing, multiplying small group effectively is a little like eating an elephant. You can't 'get it' all at once. You have to "eat it one bite at a time," learning a little more regularly and putting it into practice.

We have culled our combined sixty years of small group leadership experience to give you what we believe are the 52 most important lessons on small group leadership. If you take each lesson seriously and apply it to your ministry, you will enjoy a healthy, growing, multiplying small group.

This "small but mighty" book contains high-octane equipment, empowerment, and encouragement for any small group leader. Great for beginners, it also offers practical guidance for the most seasoned veteran. Nehemiah rebuilt the walls around Jerusalem in 52 days. You can learn to effectively lead a small group through these 52 chapters. Each one is written as a stand-alone article, yet they tie together to train, teach, and encourage small group leaders through the daily and weekly challenges all leaders face.

How to use this book effectively

The human mind typically creates vague memories and then builds on them like a pearl does with a grain of sand. Reading this pocket book more than once will give you the greatest benefit. Because of its size, it won't take long to read and then re-read. Consider the following options to get the most out of the content.

If you've been leading a group for a year or more, read the whole book straight through to get the big picture of how to lead small groups more effectively. Then, read a chapter a day for 52 days and highlight the issues you currently face as a leader. When you're done, go back through it, find the highlighted areas, and work on them one at a time.

If you're new to small group leadership, read the whole book straight through and then re-read just one chapter a week. Work hard on the application of each chapter's content throughout a calendar year and you'll become one of those special leaders that people love to follow.

If you're married, you can read this book aloud to your spouse using one of the routines above and then apply it as a team. We also recommend that you discuss what you are learning with your small group coach or pastor, other small group leaders, and with those you are mentoring as future leaders. Verbalizing the content of this book increases retention dramatically and turns fleeting ideas into lifelong ministry principles.

We pray that this little book will become more

than a book to you. May it become your pocket coach, equipping encourager, and idea catalyst.

- Dave and Rod (while enjoying looking at the mountains from Dave's back porch at the base of the Blue Ridge Mountains.)

Chapter 1

God's Big Priorities

By Dave

Everyone in our small group leader training session had been instructed to introduce themselves to five people before they sat down. Tony sheepishly extended his hand to me and with some embarrassment said, "My name is Tony. I am *just* a small group leader here."

I looked him in the eye as I shook his hand. I smiled and replied, "There is no such thing as *just* a small group leader. In God's eyes, small groups are a *big* priority and so are small group leaders."

We need each other

The heart cry of every human and the lifestyle of every follower of Jesus Christ is an overwhelming need for community. Christian community is essential to us because we were created to work together. The Apostle Paul's favorite term for the church was "the body of Christ." He emphasized that no single part could survive on its own. Every part relied on the others. In 1 Corinthians 12:21, he wrote, *"The eye cannot say to the hand, 'I don't need you!' And the head cannot say to the feet, 'I don't need you!'"*

Living a life of isolation has damaging results. Loneliness has been called the most devastating illness of our day. Phil Zambaro, a Stanford University professor writes,

> "I know of no more potent killer than isolation. There is no more destructive influence on the physical and mental health than isolation of you from me and us from them. It has been known to be the central agent in the etiology of depression, paranoid schizophrenia, rape, suicide, mass murder, and a wide variety of diseases."[1]

Our relational DNA

Our hunger for relationships is an identifying mark of our humanity. Small group experts Bill Donahue and Russ Robinson write, "God chose to embed in us a distinct kind of DNA. God created us all with a 'communal gene,' an inborn, intentional, inescapable part of what it means to be human."

They continue,

> This relational DNA or "community gene" helps explain why churches need small groups. People don't come to church simply to satisfy spiritual needs. They come internally wired with a desire for connection … their hunger for togetherness is an inescapable mark of humanity."[2]

What better way to scratch this human itch and fill this gaping need for community than through an effective small group? Learning to lead a small group where people move from isolation to connection and from loneliness to love is one of the greatest ministries on the planet!

Make no mistake about it. Your small group is a big priority. It has the power to create community and connectedness. It can foster real fellowship. Biblical fellowship involves participating in life with others to the point of knowing them, feeling their hurts, sharing their joys, and encouraging their hearts. Chuck Swindoll describes what happens when real fellowship occurs. "Fences come down. Masks come off. Welcome signs are hung outside the door. Keys to the doors of our lives are duplicated and distributed. Joys and sorrows are shared."[3]

> **Lesson #1:**
> **Your small group is a very big priority to God.**

First things first

The first thing every small group leader should know is that their small group is a BIG priority. It is vitally important. Being asked to lead a small group is one of the greatest privileges on the planet. Don't take it lightly or think yourself lowly like the young man I met at that training event. Value the opportunity and prioritize it in your schedule.

Action Points:
1. Thank God for the opportunity you have been given to be involved in a small group.

2. Determine to cooperate with God to become the best small group leader you can possibly be.

Notes:
1. Charles Swindoll, *Dropping Your Guard*, (Waco, TX, WORD, Incorporated, 1983), p. 222.
2. Bill Donahue and Russ Robinson, *Building a Church of Small Groups*, (Grand Rapids, MI; Zondervan, 2001), p. 24.
3. Swindoll, p. 22.

Chapter 2

Jesus Was a
Small Group Leader

By Dave

Those who would be the *disciples* of Jesus must practice the *disciplines* of Jesus. If we want to live as Jesus lived we must do as Jesus did. One of the main things Jesus did was invite a handful of men to be gathered together with Him in an intensive ministry-focused small group. Jesus was a small group leader. Notice carefully how Mark records the doings of Jesus:

> Jesus went up on a mountainside and called to him those he wanted, and they came to him. He appointed twelve — designating them apostles — that they might be with him and that he might send them out to preach (Mark 3:13-14).

Involvement in small group life and leadership was a primary spiritual discipline in the life of Jesus Christ. Following Jesus today means following Him into deep relationships with other believers. His pattern was gathering a few to transform the many. As has been observed, Jesus invested most of His time with twelve Jewish men so he could reach the rest of the world. The question we ask is, "If Jesus, the Son of God, chose to strategically minister to a small group, *how much more* should you and I?

Every follower of Jesus must take seriously the Great Commission.

> Therefore go and make disciples of all nations, baptizing them in the name of the Father and of the Son and of the Holy Spirit, and teaching them to obey everything I have commanded you. And surely I am with you always, to the very end of the age (Mt. 28:19-20).

The heart of the Great Commission is the call to make disciples. According to Bill Hull, "The small group is the most strategic training environment used by Christ to make the kind of disciples that glorify God."[1] We ask, "If Jesus obeyed the Great Commission by leading a small group, shouldn't we do the same?"

Lesson #2: Never forget that Jesus was a small group leader

We think of Jesus as Teacher and Healer. We learn from Him as Leader. We try to emulate Him as Example. Isn't it about time we began to study and follow Him as Small Group Leader?

Some Christians consider leading a small group to be just another program or a peripheral ministry in the church. They are sadly mistaken. The Lord Jesus Christ, the Messiah, the very Son of God, the second person of the trinity, the King of Kings and the Lord of Lords was a small group leader. Being a member of and leading a small group held a central place in His time, heart, ministry, and methodology.

When you step up to take the reins as a small group leader, realize that you are treading on sacred ground. As a small group leader, you are following in the very footsteps of Jesus Christ.

Action Points:

1. Thank God that you have been given the opportunity of following Jesus into small group leadership.

2. Determine to follow Jesus' example and rely on the power of God to lead others into transformation.

Notes
1. Bill Hull, *Jesus Christ Disciple Maker*, (Old Tappan, NJ, Fleming H. Revell, 1984), p. 235.

Chapter 3

How Many Reasons
Do You Need?

By Rod

How many reasons do you need to become a small group leader? Three, five, ten, twenty? How about just one?

In the last chapter, Dave shared Jesus' command, recorded in Matthew 28:19-20, called the Great Commission. That verse begins with, "*Go therefore and make disciples . . .*" What is the command in this passage? Well you've probably heard many times that the command is to *make* disciples, but you may not have learned the powerful way Jesus conveyed the command. There are three important parts to this passage, and you'll benefit by knowing *how* we were commanded to do it.

Go!

When Jesus commanded us to *go*, it can best be translated from the Greek to mean "in your going or as you are going." This implies, of course, that as disciples we are to go about our lives with intent and purpose. We should be rubbing elbows and shoulders with those who don't know Christ. We should be praying for them, caring for them, and eventually sharing the good news with them.

Who are you rubbing shoulders with right now that doesn't know Christ? You must lead by example. Your heart for people who do not know Christ must be easy to see and emulate.

Baptism

This one is fairly straight forward … when a person makes a decision to follow Christ, he or she should be baptized in water. Now different people have different beliefs on how baptism should take place. Some believe the person should be immersed, while others believe water should be sprinkled or poured over a person's head as a public demonstration of one's new faith in Christ. Whatever you believe, it is important that you help that new believer in Christ take a stand and identify with the death, burial, and resurrection of Christ.

Teaching

The word *teaching* as Jesus used it is best translated from the Greek as, "teaching them to *observe*." We must intentionally teach new disciples to observe the teachings of Christ. Albert Schweitzer says, "There are three ways to teach a person: the first is by example, the second is by example, and the third is … (you guessed it) by example." What most people need in order to become a mature follower of Jesus is not curriculum, but someone to watch and learn from. We all need to develop to the point in our Christian life where we can exhort others to follow our example.

Finding your motivation

After reading magazine articles and books written by experienced golfers, I learned the basics of holding a club and the fundamentals of the game. Then it became very motivating to not only read about golf, but to actually get involved and play the game. Once I started playing and playing well, then I wanted to play all the time. The same is true in regard to making disciples as a small group leader… once you learn the fundamentals of disciple-making and you improve "your game," then you want to develop disciples all the time. The key to your success is to begin practicing the principles behind the command Jesus gave us. Live your life purposely for God and lead by example.

> **Lesson #3:**
> **What most people need in order to become a mature follower of Jesus is an example. That's you!**

Action Points:

1. Who can you positively influence for the kingdom? Write their names here:

2. As you go about your work and play this week, ask God to open your eyes to see the ministry opportunities that already surround you.

Chapter 4

Just Imagine...
By Rod

Many years ago, The Temptations had a number one song entitled, *Just My Imagination*. The words to that song described the plight of a poor young man who imagined the most beautiful girl in the world was his. Can you hum or sing a few bars to that classic song? The last time I heard the song, I made an observation about the young man. He was willing to dream that the most beautiful girl in the world could be his. A true visionary!

What about you?

When it comes to the kingdom of God, what occupies your imagination? I like the quote by Marilyn Grey, "We know not where our dreams will take us, but we can probably see quite clearly where we'll go without them." Imagination has the power to stir us to action.

Let's go back to the shores of Galilee over 2,000 years ago and listen to a teacher, who was teaching with such authority that the crowds were "amazed at this teaching." This teacher was Jesus. He told his followers to go into all the world and make disciples. Can you imagine the stirring in the disciples' hearts as they heard Him say, "But you will receive power when the Holy Spirit has come upon you; and you will be My witnesses both in Jerusalem, and in all Judea and Samaria and even to the end of the earth." They may have swallowed hard and their stomachs turned just a little bit when they heard, "the end of the earth," but they were willing to dream. This was no small plan. It would require extreme commitment and sacrifice, making it hard to attain. Nevertheless, this plan stirred their imagination and they responded.

Leading small groups and developing leaders is part and parcel of accomplishing the Great Commission. It is challenging and requires spiritual sweat. But it is worth it. Imagine the joy of seeing men and women growing spiritually right before your very eyes. Now imagine seeing people turn from controlling and debilitating habits and "putting on" new thoughts and destroying speculations and every lofty thing contrary to the knowledge of God. Or imagine helping a young leader navigate the challenges of discipleship. Better still; imagine one day standing before the Lord Himself and hearing Him say, "Well done good and faithful servant. Good job!" That's what I want to hear. I want to let those words wash over me, like a warm shower on a cold morning.

**Lesson #4:
To see disciples developed, a person must get up a little earlier and go to bed a little later than most.**

In order for these things to happen, you must

not only have imagination, but be willing to take action and put feet on your dreams. To see the bright sunshine of freedom and victory over sin in the lives of others, you must become comfortable with the darkness of the prayer closet, on those days when you can only pray and seek God's face for vision and direction.

To see disciples developed, a person must get up a little earlier and go to bed a little later than most to seek God's face for vision and direction. To see immature believers become mature full-grown followers of the Master, a small group leader must see things first, farther and more clearly than others. Begin with imagination and take it a step further with some hard work and determination.

The young man in the song had a great imagination, but never ventured out to meet the girl. Had he determined to meet her instead of sing her praises from a distance, we might have heard a very different song on the radio. Become the kind of small group leader that imagines the future and works hard toward achieving it with God's power and guidance.

Action Points:

1. What goals are you setting for yourself and your small group? List them here.

2. Are you making any sacrifices to find and meet your goals? If you're not, list some things you know you should be doing on this page and tell someone so they can encourage you to follow through.

Chapter 5

Developing Others
By Rod

While attending a public high school years ago, I played sports. Even though I was a little on the small side, I played basketball in high school and one year in junior college. Basketball was my sport, but for some unknown reason — probably peer pressure or temporary insanity — I went out for the football team in the tenth grade.

What was I thinking? I had not taken the time, effort, or interest to develop muscles in that region of my body because basketball was not a brute strength sport. To excel in football, I discovered one must be able to push people around with highly developed muscles. I soon learned that without some weight training and extra meat on my bones, I was never going to be the pusher. I was just the skinny "pushee."

To excel in the spiritual arena and in small group leadership, you must also develop muscles ... *spiritual* muscles. This development takes the form of one level building upon another level and continual devotion to the right exercises in order to make progress in the spiritual dimension. I have personally been involved in developing many disciples and observed a progression for developing disciples in small groups.

Finding the cross

The first foundational level is trusting Christ as Savior. You cannot make progress in team sports unless you are on the team. 2 Peter 3:9 says that *"The Lord is not slow in keeping his promise, as some understand slowness. He is patient with you, not wanting anyone to perish, but everyone to come to repentance."* This verse seems to imply that God wants everyone to come into a relationship with Himself and to be saved. Once saved, though, God wants you to develop into the image of Christ.

Sanctification

The Bible tells us in 1 Thessalonians 4:3-4, *"It is God's will that you should be sanctified: that you should avoid sexual immorality; 4that each of you should learn to control his own body in a way that is holy and honorable,"* … and verse 7 summarizes the will of God again by saying, *"For God did not call us to be impure, but to live a holy life."* This passage makes it clear that God desires us to grow spiritually and to put aside anything that hinders our spiritual development. To be specific, spending time in the Word and prayer, memorizing Scripture and meditating on Scripture, and reflecting and recording our thoughts in a journal are all excellent habits to develop spiritual muscles. The disciplines in this second level enable us to become more like Christ and to be effective in leading small groups.

Servanthood

The Bible describes the third level us in

Mark 10:45: *"...the Son of man did not come to be served, but to serve and to give his life a ransom for many."*

Let me challenge you with a couple of questions. Where are you serving? Whom are you serving? If you are vague or fuzzy on the answers to those questions, then it's time to pray and find a need or a place to serve. Ask the Lord to open your eyes to see the needs of the members of your group and help them in some way.

Strategic servanthood

The fourth level is similar to the third and builds upon the third level, but make no mistake about it, it is a different level. The fourth level is strategic in nature. This area takes into consideration your unique talents and gifts that the Lord has given you. Do you know your spiritual gifts? What special ability do you have for ministry? Teaching, administration, serving, helps, mercy, giving ... I don't know what your primary gift is, but you better know what it is! Make sure you not only know the answer; but you are exercising your gifts for the Master.

Bearing fruit

The fifth level is found in John 15:8 where Jesus challenges us by saying, *"This is to my Father's glory, that you bear MUCH* [emphasis added mine] *fruit, showing yourselves to be my disciples."* What fruit are you producing for the Master? Hopefully you are investing in the "fruit that will remain." How are you investing in the Great Commission and how is that investment translating into the lives of people? Small groups are the best place for positive change to take place. When people get saved, they want to grow. When people grow, they want to serve. When people start serving, they want to invest strategically. When people invest strategically they begin to reap the results.

Your spiritual development

At the top level, we find the purpose of all this spiritual development. For a Christian … the reason to develop as a disciple and the reason to develop other disciples is to ultimately bring as much glory to God as possible with one's life. Theologians call this the "summa theologia." The sum of all theology is to live your life in such a way that it would ultimately bring glory to God. Getting saved, growing spiritually, serving, and producing fruit … brings glory to God. When this happens, then you are a developing disciple who is developing disciples!

Action Point:

In your small group, who is growing spiritually? How can you help them move deeper into servanthood and intimacy with God?

Chapter 6

Got G.R.O.U.P.?

By Rod

Do you remember the ad campaign entitled, "Got Milk?" The ad would appear with a well-known star sporting a milk moustache. The star, looking very debonair, would talk about the benefits of drinking milk and would always end the advertisement with the question, "Got milk?"

Let me ask you a question in my most dashing accent … "Got G.R.O.U.P.?" This is an acrostic whose letters stand for the following areas of true leadership.

Guided by a leader

Lee Roberson said, "Everything rises and falls on leadership." Simply put, if you don't have a leader it ain't going to happen. In all of my years of ministry experience this is one of the most challenging aspects of ministry. Specifically, moving a person beyond salvation, past basic spiritual growth, forward to serving, and then to strategic serving is no easy task. Leadership is not about what can you do for me, but rather what can I do for you. It begins with a heart that asks the question, "How can I help you grow and become more like Christ?"

When a small group leader understands this process, then he or she is in the business of true spiritual leadership. In order for a group to be successful, the leader of the group needs to view their role as drawing out the new creation that God has in mind for every individual in the group. When you do this, then your group is led by a true leader.

Regular meeting times

I prefer weekly, but every other week will work if you have a good way to connect with people in the off-weeks. Meeting monthly will not work if you are serious about helping the people in your group grow *and* develop. If you are meeting monthly, a person could miss one meeting and it might be a full two months before you see that person again. If you are trying to shepherd the flock of God with integrity, this is not acceptable. In two months' time, the enemy, who prowls about like a roaring lion, will easily use his tricks of deception, discouragement, and disillusionment to defeat one of your group members. Meeting weekly is best because you can adequately lead the sheep entrusted to your care and protect them as well. Meeting weekly is the bare minimum to provide the right environment for growth and development.

Open God's Word

The Bible tells us in Hebrews 4:12 that the *"...word of God is living and active. Sharper than any double-edged sword, it penetrates even to dividing soul and spirit, joints and marrow; it judges the thoughts and attitudes of the heart.* "Among the many things we do when we meet together as a small group, we must take responsibility to break

open the Word of Life. The Bible has the power to change people's lives from the inside out. Consider Romans 12:2: *"Do not conform any longer to the pattern of this world, but be transformed by the renewing of your mind. Then you will be able to test and approve what God's will is — his good, pleasing and perfect will."* Studying and applying the Word of God has the power to change us from what we are into what God has in mind for us.

United in love

In the New Commandment (John 13:34-35), Jesus exhorts us to *"Love one another. As I have loved you, so you must love one another."* The book of Acts describes the love that the early church had for each other in this way, *"They began selling their property and possessions, and were sharing them with all, as anyone might have need."* They did this to meet needs that were coming to the forefront in that early gathering of believers. While I'm not advocating a form of Christian communism, I am suggesting we adopt a radical "others first" brand of Christianity. We must sacrifice to meet the needs of others and show God's true love. Remember this truism: "People don't care how much you know until they know how much you care."

Prayer for one another

In addition to studying and applying the Word, praying for and *with* one another is what separates a Christ-centered small group from a civic club. People get together in civic settings all across the country every day. The church must be different!

What separates the church from secular groups is the spiritual content (Word of God) and spiritual encouragement (prayer). Something amazing happens every time you ask someone the question, "How can I pray for you?" It is equally amazing what happens when two or three people begin to agree on something and begin to petition our Heavenly Father (Matt. 18:19). Don't underestimate the power of small group prayer when you meet together.

Taken together, this simple acrostic can help you determine whether those you lead each week are one of God's small groups or just another civic club. So I ask you again, "Got G.R.O.U.P.?"

Action Points:

1. Are you meeting regularly with your group to pray, study the Word, and apply what you are learning?

2. What sacrifices could the members of your group make to ease the burden of another member of the group? List them below.

Chapter 7

The Five Practices of Healthy Small Groups

By Dave

"This group changed my life!"

"That's nothing," another replied, "This group *saved* my life."

I sat there and silently rejoiced as I heard one student after another tell how the weekly gathering in our home has been used of God to make a difference. I was grateful for the impact of a healthy small group in the lives of these high school students. I also thanked God for the simple, yet powerful practices that allow God to work mightily in creating a healthy small group for those who are young or just young at heart.

So why do some small groups attract and keep people, while others struggle to stay alive? Why do some grow and multiply and some do not? Is there some set of activities a small group can do to improve its health and vitality? What are the common denominators of highly potent small groups? What can be done to increase the probability that a group will grow and multiply?

If such practices exist, are they beyond the reach of the average small group and will they take years to master? Or is there a set of activities that are simple, attainable, and realistic enough that any small group that desires to be healthy can put them into their weekly gathering?

I believe there is an answer to all of these questions. I have had the privilege of leading small groups and coaching small group leaders for …gulp …almost thirty years. It began when, as a 16-year-old public school student, my friend and I started lunchtime Bible studies at our high school. They "accidentally" grew and multiplied. In college, I started a discipleship group that spread over the campus. During my summers in college I got to help start groups in little towns in England and in high rises on Manhattan in New York City.

Lesson #7:
Healthy, growing, and multiplying groups incorporate five basic practices into each weekly meeting.

When I graduated from college, I started a few groups in rural Virginia. Then I was hired to train, write curriculum, and oversee 300 small group leaders at a large Christian university. Later I started a group in my basement that grew into a church that now has over a hundred groups and has birthed several other churches.

Most of these groups became healthy. Some grew and multiplied while others did not. Through the years I noticed that the long-range effectiveness of a group revolved around some simple habits practiced during group gatherings and flowed over into the week.

While many small groups deeply desire to grow and multiply, they are not sure how to go about it. It is really not complicated at all. Let me explain.

Several years ago I wanted to help the group I led and the many groups I was overseeing become healthier. By studying cell group and small group ministry and thinking through my own experience, I identified five practices that made the difference between health and disease, effectiveness and ineffectiveness. I put them into our weekly small group agenda and the results were amazing. A new group of teens and myself grew, multiplied a few times and became a 'supergroup' of ten small groups ministering to sixty high school students a week. (While my initial success was with students, I have found the five practices work with adults just as well.)

I began by asking the leaders I coached to adopt these habits and build them into their weekly gatherings. Without exception, those who adopted and practiced these habits became much healthier groups. And those who did not ... well, they did not.

I am so excited about the simple beauty and potential power of these practices because they really do work. Following the five practices of an effective small group makes all the difference between mediocrity and greatness, between routine faithfulness and dynamic fruitfulness, between stagnation and multiplication. Practicing them also allows God to increase His transformational activity in the group.

The best quality about these practices is that they are doable. Any group can incorporate these practices into their weekly agenda and begin to see powerful results. In the chapters to follow, I will explain each practice in detail and give you a practical understanding of how to implement each one.

Applying these five practices will take your group to a new level. They are a path to group health and group. With this in mind, make mental notes as you read the next few pages and work hard to incorporate what you learn.

Action points:

1. Ask God to help your group become more healthy and effective at loving each other by practicing transparency during your upcoming meetings.

2. Read the next six chapters in order to learn more about the five practices.

Chapter 8

Welcome: The Basics for Building Great Community

By Dave

Neal McBride has wisely noted an obvious, yet often overlooked reality when he writes,

> Not all groups are really groups. Some are merely a collection of individuals with the appearance of a group... The members assume that by calling themselves a group, they become one.[1]

One of the primary purposes, passions, and practices of the healthy small group is developing community. The Bible supplies the clearest guidelines for how to develop community in your group. Small groups will experience dynamic community by obeying the "one another" commands found in the New Testament. If you have your Bible handy, read each verse and then come back to the text of each one for my comments. This will help you tie what you are reading to a new understanding of the "one another" passages.

Love each other *(Jn. 13:34)*
Love is the beginning, middle, and end of

Christian community. Love, of course, is the foundation on which the other "one another" commands are built. Love is also the oil that lubricates the process. If you remember nothing else from this chapter, remember this: "Love one another." The rest of the "one another commands" tell us *how* to love another in small group life.

Move beyond your comfort zone to affectionately greet one another *(Rom. 16:16; 1 Cor. 16:20; 2 Cor. 13:12; 1 Peter 5:14)*

Good groups start with members greeting one another. It breaks the ice and lowers defenses. Greeting is especially of the utmost importance during the first few sessions of a new group as it forms.

We live in a high tech, low touch world. One major reason people get involved in a group is they want a safe, high touch environment. Learn to use the time of greeting as members arrive or after they have all arrived to greet one another with an appropriate touch. In some cultures this would be a handshake. In other cultures, it's a hug. In still others, it's a kiss.

Lesson #8: Small groups build community by following the "one another" commands.

Remember: As touch goes up, defenses come down and receptivity increases.

Hold each other in high esteem and actively honor one another *(Rom. 12:16)*

After a group has been birthed, it grows into childhood in its second and third month. This is a time of testing as members learn what is and isn't acceptable as group members. This is a key time to remind the group of behavioral guidelines, especially that of honoring one another.

Nothing builds community more than the atmosphere of esteem and honor. When a group breathes an atmosphere of respect and regard, meaningful, authentic relational community will grow.

Group members can show one another respect by cutting out cut-downs, wisecracks, and talking when someone else is speaking. Members need to show esteem by giving others their undivided attention. Members must celebrate the joys of the others and seriously consider their questions and struggles.

Accept one another *(Rom. 15:7; 14:13)*

When people sense a spirit of criticism or self-righteousness in others, they either close down or look for faults in others as a defense mechanism. A spirit of criticism will draw the life out of a community. On the other hand, unconditional acceptance becomes fertile soil to foster deep relationships. Give others the freedom to be themselves.

Encourage one another *(1 Th. 5:11; Heb. 3:13; 10:25)*

The word encouragement speaks of "coming

alongside of another to give them courage." Living for God in a godless world can be a fearful challenge. Everyone needs a team behind them saying, "You can do it. Don't quit." Encouragement is oxygen for the soul.

Move your group beyond being a collection of people and into a biblical community or an interconnected body of believers with what you've learned in this chapter.

Action Points:

1. Be certain every person is greeted warmly and appropriately every time your group meets, even if they arrive after the meeting has begun.

2. Use an icebreaker question every week, especially when you have visitors. This focuses the group members on each other.

3. When a group is new, spend a large percentage of your group time building community and getting to know one another.

Notes:
1. Neal McBribe, *Real Small Groups Don't Just Happen*, (Colorado Springs, Colorado, NavPress, 1998), p.11

Chapter 9

Maintaining Community

By Dave

Once a group has gelled and the members love each other, the job of building and maintaining community is not finished. It has only just begun. The "one another" commands of the New Testament show us how community is maintained. In the last chapter, I explored five key passages. In this chapter, I'll continue by showing you *how* the "one another" commands can be practically implemented.

Make the effort to resolve conflict *(Rom. 12:16)*

During the first few months of getting to know one another, conflicts may arise. Yet the potential for conflict is always present. No two people are alike. Therefore, it is just a matter of time until there is a rift between members. To try to deny or avoid variance is to kill true community. To resolve it *builds* community. When conflict comes — and it will come — the healthy group will work to resolve it and live in harmony. Here are a few basics to move you through conflict.

First, pray for discernment. Ask yourself, "Is there really a conflict or am I just being overly sensitive?" Many choose to take offense where the person in question simply chose the wrong words or could have phrased what they said in a better way. One must always look at the intent of the other person before assuming he or she meant harm with what was done or said.

Second, determine to own your part of the problem. Many conflicts are two sided and the action of the other person is actually a *reaction* to something you may have done or said.

Third, determine the best time to talk privately with the person, which may be right away. Or, you may need to wait until you are calm and have collected your thoughts. But don't wait too long. In either case, begin by letting them know that this might not be a comfortable conversation, but it is an important one.

Lesson #9: Small groups maintain community by resolving conflict and walking in humility.

If you have been the primary source of offense, I recommend that you make your approach using some form of these twelve simple words for resolving conflict. I am not sure where I first heard them, but I have used them frequently with great success. They are: "I was wrong;" "I am sorry;" "Please forgive me;" and "I love you."

If the other person is the primary source of offense, you need to begin by affirming the value of your relationship by communicating that the reason you want to resolve this conflict is because you care about your relationship. Then share what you have observed in terms of what was seen, heard, and felt. Don't make accusations. Ask the person how he or she perceived the situation. Then try to gain a mutual understanding.

Bear with each other and forgive one another
(Eph. 4:32)

Community means "being family." This is expressed by loving all the people all the time, no matter what they are going through, regardless if they are having a bad day or are enduring a challenging set of circumstances. Community is deepened as you go with them through those times and continue to bear with them, and when necessary, forgive them.

Submit to one another *(Eph. 5:21)*

When it comes to preferences, arguments are not worth winning. Don't try to win every argument or always be right. In the big scheme of life, it probably won't make any difference. Community grows when you are willing to submit to one another and "agree to disagree" on preferential issues.

Refuse to slander someone in or outside the group
(Jas. 4:11)

Nothing will shut down community more quickly than slander. Most of us could tell horror stories of group life that was short-circuited by slander or gossip. It is wise to remind people every week that your small group is a safe place to share deep feelings. "What is said here stays here" is a good phrase that says it all. Once group members know that this is a true statement, sharing will deepen and community will grow.

Take turns showing hospitality to one another
(1 Peter 4:9)

Don't let hospitality be the job of just one person or couple. The enemy is quick to move in and create hard feelings when the load of hospitality is not recognized, appreciated, and shared. For this reason, many wise groups rotate the people who bring the snacks and others who open their homes for group meetings.

Clothe yourself in a servant's apron of humility
(1 Peter 5:5)

There is no such thing as a community of one. Often, gifted teachers build groups on their awesome teaching, but the community life of the group suffers because the group revolves around the teacher. Or, there are those folks who think of the group as their personal counseling session and repeatedly monopolize the sharing time with lengthy stories of their never-ending problems. A good guideline for any group is "everyone participates, no one dominates."

Sin dulls light and destroys fellowship *(1 Jn. 1:7)*

The deception and masks created by sin are a real community killer. True community is built through honest confession to one another and prayer for one another. Don't expect your small group members to confess their deepest sins in the meetings. The confession of sin is typically done one-on-one with another member of the group outside the meeting. This is why helping each person in your group form an accountable relationship with another one or two people of the same sex in the group is so important.

Motivate one another *(Heb. 10:24)*

Encourage each other to do the right things in life and ministry. God-hungry people bond with those who lovingly challenge them to get out of their comfort zones and go deeper, higher, and further for God. Some of this can be done in meetings, but once again, the one on one relationship that motivates by loving encouragement and servanthood is the most powerful.

Action Point:

For the next few weeks in your group, talk about how you can apply these "one another" commands of Jesus. Be specific with the application and challenge the group to actually do what they're discussing and report back to the group with the results.

Chapter 10

Worship: Never Neglect the Power of Exalting God

By Dave

For several years, we led a large group of high school students in our house. Most of them were non-churched. It was always amazing how wonderfully they behaved. They often came in rowdy and loud. Yet, our time of worship never failed to quiet them down and prepare them for the Word. Only heaven knows how many were saved and eternally changed because of their initial encounters with God through worship.

One of the greatest, yet simple reasons groups fail to reach their potential is they neglect the power of worship. Never neglect the life-changing power of the presence of God available through worship. Let's not get ahead of ourselves here. Let's begin with the basic question … why worship?

Worship is a moral obligation and a natural response to the absolute worth of God

In other words, we worship God because he is *worth it*. God is great and greater than anyone or anything we can imagine. God has done great things for us. We should constantly remind ourselves of this by worshipping him.

Worship completes us

In Isaiah 43:21, God refers to us as His people He formed *"for myself that they may proclaim my praise."* God created us to be proclaimers of His praise, to be worshippers. Until we become worshippers, we are not fulfilling our purpose for existence. When we fail to fulfill this purpose, we will fail to be fulfilled.

Worship is transforming

2 Corinthians 3:18 says, *"And we, who with unveiled faces all reflect the Lord's glory, are being transformed into his likeness with ever-increasing glory, which comes from the Lord..."* The word Christian means "little Christ." The goal of the Christian is to become more like Christ. Becoming like Christ is a process that takes time. We all know that we tend to become like the people with whom we associate. Worship is high-level hanging around with Jesus. Therefore, it is life changing.

Lesson #10: Worship invites Christ to work in your midst. Give it priority in your group.

Worship puts life back into perspective

Psalm 73 is the journal entry of David getting out of perspective. He is struggling with the seeming prosperity of the wicked. How can they be wicked and prosper? Then in verse 16 he writes,

When I tried to understand all this, it was oppressive to me till I entered the sanctuary of God; then I understood ... God is the strength of my heart and my portion forever ... But as for me, it is good to be near God (Psalm 73:16-17, 26, 28).

What happened in the sanctuary that changed his perspective and encouraged his heart? Worship is what happened in the sanctuary. David focused on God.

Worship intensifies the presence and therefore the activity of God

Psalm 22:3 can be understood as teaching that God's address is praise, *"Yet you are enthroned as the Holy One; you are the praise of Israel."* I have found that God often manifests His presence in proportion to our expressed recognition of our need and love for Him. Jesus promised in Matthew 18:20 *"For where two or three come together in my name, there am I with them."*

Now that we know why we should worship, the next logical question would be how to worship effectively. In a nutshell, worship is a verb. Worship is not something done to us, or for us, but by us. More than a feeling, it is a choice or an action. Worship is something we must do. You can use music and sing, but you don't have to have music to worship. You can truly worship by practicing various forms of non-musical group prayer. The goal is to actively worship God regularly in your daily devotional times and in every small group gathering.

Action Point:

A study of the Bible reveals over a dozen responses involved in worshipping God. Pick a few and build the reading of them into your next meeting's worship time.

1. Being silent in awe (Isa. 6).
2. Kneeling or laying face down in absolute surrender (Rev. 4).
3. Confessing sin (2 Samuel 12; Ps. 51).
4. Shouting in thanksgiving (Ps. 42:4; 66:1-2; 100:1; 71:23; 98:4).
5. Trembling in reverence (Rev. 5:8).
6. Resolving to obey (Gen. 22).
7. Praising in the midst of difficulties (Job 1).
8. Giving God offerings out of gratitude (2 Sam. 24, 1 Kings 8; 2 Chron. 5-6).
9. Yielding your will (Jnh. 2).
10. Dancing (2 Sam. 6; Ps. 149:3).
11. Singing for joy (Ex. 15; Ps. 21:13; 63:5; 71:22).
12. Playing musical instruments (Ps. 43:4; 71:22; 98:4-6).
13. Clapping your hands (Ps. 47:1).
14. Lifting your hands (Ps. 63:4; 134:2).

Chapter 11

Witness: How to Be a People-Reaching Group

By Dave

Any small group that possesses a passion for reaching people for Christ will be successful if they follow a few basic practices. For example, the group my family led for a few years started with a handful of youth and eventually grew to over 50 high school students meeting in one house (in six groups) and another fifteen students meeting at a second home. The best thing about this is that dozens of unchurched young people found Jesus as a result of our small groups. It was one of the most fulfilling and fun groups I ever led.

In the years since that time, I have stuck to these basic practices with every small group I've lead and coached, including many adult groups. You might be thinking it grew because members of the group were students, but that's not the case. We were effective because we intentionally practiced ten keys that allowed us to reach people for Christ.

Faith

We believed that God wanted people saved more than we did. Therefore, all we had to do was cooperate with Him. We developed a strong expectation that if we invited people, they would come. We also decided that if we shared the gospel, they would respond. Of course, not every member of the group did these things, but enough responded to cause us to believe that God honored our efforts.

Prayer

Evangelism is a spiritual war that is best fought on one's knees. As long as we were *consistently* praying that God would save souls, He did! Before events where the gospel was to be presented, we intensified our prayers and God always granted a harvest.

Love

Evangelism is a relational process involving three successive victories: First, we won people to ourselves. Second, we won people to our group. Third, we won people to Christ. Lots of believers wonder why they cannot win people to Christ and it's because they don't win them as a true friend first.

Invitation

If you invite them, they might come. But if you don't invite them, they'll probably never come. Unsaved people rarely just drop into a group on their own. A vast majority of the time, one or more members of the group made the effort to invite them.

T.E.A.M. (Together Everyone Accomplishes More)

It's corny, but true! Periodically, we would ask

various group members to share how they came to our group. With only a few exceptions, each person shared how they were invited by *four or five group members* before they decided to give it a try.

Gospel

Never underestimate the power of the gospel. Every four to six weeks we would share the story of the death, burial, and resurrection of Jesus for our sins. We would also share that you can be saved by admitting your sins, believing on Christ for salvation, calling on his name to save you, and committing your life to Him. Without exception, people responded.

Lesson #11: You must be intentional about winning people to your group and to Christ.

Process

Evangelism is a process leading to an event. Few people are ready to give their lives to God the first time they are invited to group. I taught my small group members to be patient, helping them understand it takes weeks, months, and even years of inviting, praying, loving, and hearing the Word before the soil is ready to yield a harvest.

Party

Never underestimate the power of a party to draw a crowd! Every two months, we planned social gatherings. Amongst ourselves we jokingly called them "sinner dinners." We found that we could double our attendance and get non-churched students to come to our house if the kids invited them to a "party." We have found if we have a theme ("Squirt Gun Wars," "I Hate Winter," "Halloween Bonfire," and "Fifties Night" are always hits), grill some hot dogs, and play a few corny games, we'll have a crowd. They will have a blast and will listen intently to a few of their friends share their story of how they came to a personal relationship with Jesus. We have had as many as eighty-nine kids show up and as many as a dozen make salvation decisions for Christ—all because we had a party. Adults enjoy parties too. You'd be surprised how many of your group's friends will come to a game night or get together to watch a movie. Just remember that guests love to contribute, so ask them to bring something tasty with them and they'll instantly feel at home at the gathering.

Testimony

One of the easiest ways to gain attention, sustain interest, and preach the gospel without being "preachy" in your small group meetings is to have someone share how they came to Christ. It is wise to have a testimony that somewhat mirrors the people you hope to reach. For example, if you are inviting unsaved husbands to your group have a former unsaved husband share how he came to Christ.

Celebration

In Luke 15, we find three stories of something lost being found; a lost sheep (vv. 1-7), a lost coin

(vv. 8-10), and a lost son (vv.11-31). In each case, the event was marked by a celebration. Maybe God would give us more opportunities to win the lost if we truly rejoiced when one was found. The celebration can be as simple as cheering for and hugging the new believer or as big as a full-blown party. How you celebrate is not as important as the fact that you celebrate.

Action Point:

Pick a few of these practices to become a people-reaching group. Then start incorporating them into your group until people are consistently coming to Christ.

Chapter 12

Word: Bible Study, Discussion, and Application Basics

By Dave

If community is the glue of your group, worship is the heart, and evangelism the fruitful mission, then the foundation of the group is your weekly time spent together in the Word of God.

Do not underestimate the power of the Word of God. Among other things, the Bible is the bestselling, most read, studied, and memorized book in the world. It is also the most published book in the world, currently available in 1,500 languages. It is also the world's most quoted, cussed, and discussed book. History reveals that it is the most influential book ever written and the most unstoppable, indestructible book ever written. It has inspired more songs, poems, and other books than any other. Archeology shows that the Bible is the most reliable ancient text known to man. Fulfilled prophecy makes it the most unique book on the planet. Careful reading shows it to be the most honest, accurate, and interesting religious book ever penned. Because it is God's Word, the Bible is by far the most important book imaginable.

The point of the Bible and the reward for reading it is more than just to know interesting facts about what one finds within it. It is to know God and His plan for our lives. It is written so you and I can become transformed or changed into His image. It is also there for us so we can be better equipped to make a difference in the world.

Bible Study Basics

In studying a passage of the Bible there are three basic questions we must always ask.

What does this passage say?

This is the act of *Observation*. Read the passage through while asking, "What does this passage seem to be saying? What is the author saying? Who wrote this passage? To whom was he writing? Why was he writing?

What does this passage mean?

This is the act of *Interpretation*. Take each passage in chunks of phrases, sentences, or paragraphs. As you look at it, answer the question: "What did the author intend for this to mean?" Try to paraphrase it into your own words.

How can we apply this passage to our lives?

This is the act of *Application*. Interpretation without application leads to spiritual abortion, but interpretation with application leads to transformation. Lead every member of the group to be able to finish this sentence: "Based on what this says, I should...." Responses may be in terms of a sin to confess, a promise to claim, an example you need to follow, an encouragement to accept, or a command for you to keep.

Bible Discussion Basics

Good leaders always help the members of their group discover biblical truths for themselves. Therefore they lead a discussion rather than preach a sermon. There are four major types of questions to aid this process:

1. Introducing the Discussion

Learn to ask a question or questions that will lead the group members into the scripture or the topic of study and "break the ice" between members. For example, during a discussion on the Ten Commandments you could ask:

- Who laid down the law in your family?
- Why do parents make rules?
- Which rule did you like the least?
- Which family member tried to get around the rules? How?
- What were the consequences of breaking the rules?[1]

> **Lesson #12:**
> **Make the study and practical application of God's Word a central focus of your group.**

2. Guiding the Discussion

The point of these questions is to dig deeper into the passage. Some examples would be:

- What did you feel as you read these words?

- Why do you think God put this passage in the Bible?
- Who will paraphrase this passage in their own words?
- Who else would like to comment on that?

During this time, helping the group get back on track may be required. If your group starts "chasing rabbits," say something like, "That's very interesting, but we're off topic. Let's get back to the passage."

3. *Summarizing the Discussion*

One of the most important roles of a group leader is summarizing the discussion so the group will be able to apply it at a later date. You may ask the group such questions as, "We have been having a very good discussion. Who will try to summarize the main things we are learning (or we have said) in just one or two sentences?" Another way to help the group summarize is to ask, "If a stranger rang the door bell and asked you what our group discussed tonight, what would you say?" Then keep the discussion going by asking, "Who else? Would you say anything different or in addition to what he (or she) said?"

4. *Applying the Discussion*

Application questions can be the most powerful part of your discussion. Help each member of the group verbalize how they will apply the Bible passage to their lives. Ask such questions as:

a. What one thing that was discussed tonight do you want to remember all week?

b. Specifically, how will your life be different this week because we studied this passage tonight?

c. What do you hope to do differently or more of based on what we talked about tonight?

d. In light of what we've learned tonight, does anyone here have anything they'd like to confess or share with the group?

Build your group on a firm foundation of the Word of God. Study it, discuss it, and most importantly, *apply* the Word to your lives!

Action Point:

1. Take what you've learned in this chapter and apply it to your next week's small group study and application time.

2. Then, take five minutes at the end of the meeting to ask the group if they saw any differences and what they thought of the changes, if any were made.

Notes
1. *Serendipity Bible for Groups*, (Serendipity House, Littleton, CO. 1988), has many helpful icebreaker questions.

Chapter 13

Works: Ministry Matters

By Dave

When Cathy and I graduated from college, my parents gave us one of the greatest presents we have ever received. They helped us by paying for a trip to the Holy Land. One of the images I remember best is that of the Dead Sea. It is a bizarre place close to where Sodom and Gomorrah are believed to have been. The Dead Sea is actually a large lake fed primarily by the Jordan River.

The Dead Sea is also called the Salt Sea. It is surrounded by cliffs and is the deepest body of water on earth. It is so dark it is almost black in color. It is saltier than the ocean. The reason it is called the Dead Sea is because there is almost no organic life in its waters.

I will never forget trying to go for a swim in the Dead Sea. The water is so thick it was like wearing a life jacket. You can practically sit on the surface of the water. When you get out of the water, you are covered with a greasy, salty film that feels gross. Why? While it is a very deep body of water, it's also very dead because it has no outlet.

Because of that amazing experience overseas, God has taught us me a profound spiritual principle. Too many small group members are like the Dead Sea. They take in rich deposits of truth and have become very deep. Yet they are stagnant and spiritually dead. Why? Just like the Dead Sea, they have no outlet because they never get involved in ministry.

When I use the word *ministry*, I am using it as the Bible does, referring to acts of service. It speaks of the service we give in our group, to our group members, and through our group to others.

Facts About Effective Ministry

Every group member is a minister

In chapter ten, I wrote how the word *Christian* means "little Christ." It means that we are to be like Jesus. What was Jesus like? Jesus described Himself this way: *"For even the Son of Man did not come to be served, but to serve, and to give his life as a ransom for many"* (Mk. 10:45). Notice the words *serve* and *give*. Ministry, serving, and giving are characteristics of the true followers of Jesus Christ.

Every ministry is important

Paul likened the church to a body. Notice the similarities. *"As it is, there are many parts, but one body. The eye cannot say to the hand, 'I don't need you!' And the head cannot say to the feet, 'I don't need you!' On the contrary, those parts of the body that seem to be weaker are indispensable"* (1 Cor. 12:20-22).

Every part is necessary. Therefore, every part has dignity. There are no insignificant parts, and there are no insignificant ministries. Real ministry is a lifestyle. Some of the personal ministries in your group could include praying daily for missionaries, watching the neighbor's kids after school, tutoring at-risk inner-city children, teaching English as a second language, or helping an elderly person by doing his or her yard work.

Every group has numerous ministries that are not always noticed, but are highly important for the weekly meeting. There is cleaning of the house, preparing of the snacks, caring for the children, leading worship, and preparing the icebreaker. We can pray for other group members daily. Take meals when one is ill. Visit them in the hospital when it is needed. Help other members of your group move furniture, or paint their house, or remodel their basement.

Beyond that, every church has a plethora of unnoticed ministries: helping weekend service attendees with parking their cars, running the audio and video board for the worship team and pastor, ushering, greeting, setting up chairs, praying before and during the worship services, changing diapers in the nursery, teaching preschoolers, sponsoring teenagers, counting the offering, folding bulletins, and answering phones, just to name a few! All are often overlooked, but very important.

> **Lesson #13: Healthy small group leaders engage their members in ministry.**

There are no unimportant servanthood ministries. Every single one is vital to the success of a small group and a church.

Every ministry is enhanced when shared with others

One of the best bonding tools for your group is to serve together. It is often a great deal of fun. Some groups work together to feed the homeless once a month. Others get together to clean a widow's yard or watch children so single moms can have a night out. Some roof a member's house. Others help someone clean up a basement or a yard after a bad storm. Some help build houses for the poor.

How your group serves does not matter as much as actually doing something, and doing it together. Every group and every group member needs a ministry outlet so they don't become like the Dead Sea.

Action Point:

1. Take notice and appreciate the ministries your group members carry out each week.

2. Make a schedule of some ministry projects your group can do together in the next three months to strengthen the team and give each person an outlet.

Chapter 14

Open Your Group!
By Rod

I like the quote by Yogi Berra, "You've got to be very careful if you don't know where you're going, because you might not get there." This is especially true in small group ministry. When we are not clear on where we want to go, we just wander around like Moses in the wilderness.

Is your group working hard to include new members as well as disciple the existing people in the group? Open groups — when fully understood — give each member a sense of purpose and direction. To lead an effective open group, you must start out with a clear mental picture of your end result and then work hard to make that end result a reality. Check out the diagram below, which illustrates how this works.

$$A \longrightarrow I \longrightarrow I \longrightarrow I \longrightarrow I \longrightarrow B$$

"A" is your point of origin or where you are today. "B" is clearly where you want to go. As you imagine your destination (the "I's" between), it must be "cloudless" in your mind before you begin. This is the kind of vision clarity required for this journey.

Personally, I believe the most effective and healthy groups maintain an emphasis on multiply-

**Lesson #14:
For your group to be open to the unsaved, you'll have to develop a clear vision for it for it to become a reality.**

ing leaders and forming new groups from the existing group. In order to accomplish this strategy, you must keep a real clear focus on the harvest fields (your vision). You must emphasis that groups are not here to just minister to "us four and no more," but effective, growing groups are here to reach out to the people who are not yet here.

Jesus had this to say about the harvest in John 4:35, *"Do you not say, 'Four months more and then the harvest'? I tell you, open your eyes and look at the fields! They are ripe for harvest."* There is a time for discipleship, but doesn't true discipleship involve evangelism and reaching out to the lost and hurting? Open groups help maintain a focus on the priority of winning people to Christ now. The Bible tells us in 2 Corinthians 6:2, *"I tell you, NOW is the time of God's favor, NOW is the day of salvation"* (emphasis mine).

When your vision is clear … then your members can follow you. Make sure that you as the leader see it first, farther and clearer than anyone else! When you have a clear picture of where you want to go and how you want to get there, then there is no stopping what you can accomplish. Open groups will also enable you to develop not just disciples, but *leaders*, which are disciplers of disciples.

Action Points:

1. Brainstorm a few intermediate steps to move your group into an open group that actively pursues relationships with unsaved persons. If you get stuck, simply ask your group to help you with your first steps when you next meet.

2. Each day, ask the Lord to open your eyes and the eyes of your members to the harvest fields of people who are desperate to know Him.

Chapter 15

Why Have a
Multiplying Group?

By Rod

When you think of difficult tasks, what comes to mind? Becoming a violin virtuoso? Competing in the Olympics? Building a house with your own hands? Having a great marriage? Raising kids? Maybe it is patting your head and rubbing your stomach at the same time! There are many difficult challenges in the world today. Life is not easy.

When it comes to the church, one of the most difficult challenges that Great Commission-driven leaders face is the challenge of not only growing a quality group, but multiplying a healthy group. In the Bible, the goal of multiplication is clear. Consider these ten passages:

1. Gen. 1:28 says, *"God blessed them and said to them, "Be fruitful and increase in number; fill the earth and subdue it. Rule over the fish of the sea and the birds of the air and over every living creature that moves on the ground."*
2. Gen. 17:2 — When Abraham is 99 years old, God gives him this promise: *"I will confirm my covenant between me and you and will greatly increase your numbers."*

3. Gen. 22:17 — God appears to Abraham again at the offering of Isaac and says, *"I will surely bless you and make your descendants as numerous as the stars in the sky and as the sand on the seashore."*

4. Gen. 26:4 — God appears to Isaac and gives the same promise to him, *"I will make your descendants as numerous as the stars in the sky and will give them all these lands..."*

5. Gen. 35:11 — God reiterates the promise to Jacob after Jacob wrestles and prevails with the Angel of the Lord and says, *"I am God Almighty; be fruitful and increase in number. A nation and a community of nations will come from you..."*

6. Matt. 14:13-21; Mk. 6:34-44; Lk. 9:12-17; and Jn. 6:5-13 — The feeding of the 5,000 is based upon the miracle of multiplication. The only way to feed, to shepherd, and to care for the multitudes is through the miracle of multiplication.

7. Mt. 15:32-39 and Mk. 8:1-9 — The Feeding of the 4,000 is based upon the miracle of multiplication. It is interesting to note that this miracle was repeated twice by Jesus. Also the "feeding of the 5,000" is recorded in all four Gospels. The "feeding of the 4,000" is recorded in Matthew and Mark. Thus, six passages (47 verses) are devoted to the miracle of multiplication.

8. Mk. 4:1-34 — In the parable of the soils, there are four types of soil: wayside soil, rocky soil, thorny soil, and receptive soil. If the Word of God finds good soil, the result is that it will yield a crop that multiplies *"thirty-fold, sixty-fold, and a hundred-fold."*

9. In Jn. 15:8 Jesus said, *"This is to my Father's glory, that you bear much fruit..."* The analogy is simple: if you abide in Christ, you will bear a multiplicity of fruit.
10. Acts 6:1; 7 — The number of disciples was growing exponentially. The New King James version translates the word 'plethuno' as "was multiplying" and 'eplethuneto' in verse 7 as "multiplied greatly." The only way to reach the world and make disciples of all the nations is through multiplication.

It is unmistakable from these passages that multiplication was God's plan for blessing His people in the Old Testament and for expanding His church in the New Testament. Could it be that multiplication is still God's plan for reaching the world and making disciples of all nations? I believe it is. The world is growing at an exponential rate, and any system or structure that is not based upon an exponential growth strategy is destined to fail.

That is why we must all work hard to develop small groups (and churches) that multiply. When small group multiplication takes place, we are fulfilling God's original intent to "be fruitful and to multiply." When you as a leader develop your group to the point where it multiplies, you will experience the

> **Lesson #15: Multiplying leaders and groups is the most rewarding part of small group leadership.**

blessing and joy of spiritual birth. There's nothing quite like seeing people you've nurtured and helped along the way take their own group.

Action Points:

1. Read through the scriptures and then the written notes in this chapter and list the ways God blesses those who have a heart for multiplication.

2. At your next meeting, ask your members to think about what your group would be like in a couple of years from today if no one left to start a new group and the membership remained the same. Would it still be a good group? Would it be boring? Would it be achieving God's amazing plans for your lives? (This is one good way to talk about who could lead a group in the future and how to move toward that goal).

Chapter 16

The Three Leadership Positions in a Small Group

By Rod

When you think of "leadership," what is the first thing that pops into your mind? Is it a military leader charging the hill, or a business leader who is bravely charting a new course of action? Perhaps you think of a coach inspiring the team to win a tough game. Maybe you think of your Mom or your Dad, who sacrificed and prayed for you … I know I do. Whatever your picture of leadership is, here are a few definitions of leadership that I have picked up over the years:

"Leadership is the processes of helping people do the worthwhile things they want to do."

- Anonymous

"Leaders have two important characteristics: first, they are going somewhere; second, they are able to persuade other people to go with them."

- Anonymous

"Leaders must know where they are going, why they are going there, and how to get there."

- Elmer Towns

"A leader is a quality person, who knows where he is going, and how to take others with him and beyond him."   *- Dave Earley*

"A spiritual leader is a quality person who knows God (and His ways) and influences others to do great things for God's glory."   *– Rod Dempsey*

I have over 60 different definitions of leadership in my files, but leadership eventually comes down to one word. That word is *influence*. In a small group environment there are at least three people who have tremendous influence on whether or not the groups are going to be successful.

The Small Group Leader

As stated previously, "everything rises and falls on leadership." In order for a group to grow, develop disciples, and to eventually birth a new group … the group must have someone who understands something about spiritual leadership. Spiritual leadership is not the same as secular leadership. Secular leadership has a tendency to view people as resources and assets to accomplish objectives. Spiritual leaders understand that their job is to develop people to their full potential in Christ. There is a growth process involved in the life of every disciple, but it is our job to serve them and empower them to "be all they can be" for Christ. The small group leader selects the curriculum if not supplied by the church, finds a good location to meet, and chooses an apprentice who will be trained to start a new group. He or she also leads the whole process toward accomplishing the goal of multiplication. It's no small task.

The Small Group Apprentice

This position is basically a small group leader in training. I've never been a big fan of the title, "Small Group Assistant." An assistant just helps the leader and perhaps fills in when the leader is absent without much thought given to leading a group of his or her own one day soon. Not so with an apprentice. An apprentice is serving under the supervision of a leader with a view of becoming a leader in a matter of months. Therefore, he or she is involved in all aspects of the group life and leadership (including a relationship to the group's coach and small group pastor) because soon they will be leading their own group.

> **Lesson #16: With the right leadership team, your group can be a powerful force to draw people to the cross and to grow in Christ.**

The Small Group Host

Integral to the effective function of any small group is the host. Usually, this is a married couple (or one or two committed single people). In a pinch, the small group apprentice(s) can serve as the host, but it is preferable to have different persons or couples providing leadership in the different areas. The host or hosts are friendly and welcoming to members and visitors coming into their homes. They may oversee the refreshment or snack schedule for the group. They also make sure there is a good location for the group to meet with enough chairs for everyone. They are vital to making the small group experience a good one for everyone who comes to their home. Should the group move to other member's homes, the host(s) should show up early to the meeting, help the home-owners arrange the chairs or set up refreshments, and welcome the members and visitors as they arrive.

The Importance of the Three Roles

Small groups are a very difficult and challenging undertaking. However, with the right leadership team they can be a very powerful force for drawing unbelievers to the cross and to grow in Christ. If you understand these leadership positions and ask the right people in your group to serve in these roles, you're well on your way to influencing others to follow Christ.

Action Points:

1. From the definitions of a leader found here, which one is your favorite? Share it with your coach or pastor and tell them *why* you like it so much.

2. Who do you need to add or develop for you small group leadership team? Write down their names and visit with your coach or pastor as to how to best work with them.

Chapter 17

What is a L.I.F.E. Group?
By Rod

There are many facets of a healthy small group. There are things that you do outside the group that make it healthy and there are things that you do in each meeting to greatly enhance group life. In this chapter, I'd like to take a look at the things you do inside the group to keep it healthy.

To help you remember the important components of inside the group life, I am going to use another acrostic called L.I.F.E. It is easy to remember because it is organic in nature. All living organisms, if they are healthy have animation and vibrancy. The same is true for small groups.

Love

There are so many exhortations to love one another in the New Testament that any group that does not have love as its main goal needs to reconsider its priorities. Consider for just a moment the following passages:

- The Great Commandment in Mark 12:33 — Jesus teaches us that we should love God with all our heart, soul, and mind and that we should love our neighbor as ourselves.

- The New Commandment in John 13:34 — In this passage, Jesus again instructs us "to love one another." He goes on to say that by our Christian love for each other all men would know that we are his disciples. Francis Schaefer wrote that our love for one another is the ultimate and final apologetic (which means our defense or answer for our beliefs).

- All the other "one anothers." — There are over 30 passages in the New Testament that contains the phrase, "one another." These passages encourage us to pray for, love, admonish, comfort, forgive, exhort, show hospitality, and so on. These "one anothers" show believers how to practice Biblical love.

Instruction

At some point, the leader of the group will open the Word of God and teach or share what God has been teaching him or her. The goal of this instruction is to draw out what God is doing in the group member's lives and how God's grace is effective in the life of the believer. If you can help your group members verbalize what God is doing in their lives, then you have helped them take a giant leap forward in the area of spiritual growth.

Fellowship

Intrinsic to group life is food, fun, and fellowship. Make sure you check out one of the chapters in this book that is devoted to the power of a party! There are dozens of fun things that you can do as a group to facilitate your group coming together. Most people don't need much of a reason to have fun, but as a leader you need to make sure that you are creatively giving them that opportunity. Here are a few examples: have a picnic together, go to a ball game together, go out to eat together after church, have a pool party together, watch the Super Bowl together … there are lots of things to do. Just make sure you do them *together*.

Lesson #17: When your group has both health and balance, it will have life.

Example

Larry Osborne is the Pastor of North Coast Church in San Diego. His explanation of the process of discipleship is brief and to the point: "Your job as a small group leader is to glue people to the Word of God and to relationships and the Holy Spirit will take care of the rest." This approach minimizes your part and maximizes the role and the importance of examples and the Holy Spirit. You are here, as a leader, to create the right "ecosystem" for spiritual growth to take place. Lead by example.

As a small group leader, if you are faithful in creating a small group context that has L.I.F.E., then you will see people growing and becoming more like Christ. When you have health and balance, you have life!

Action Points:

1. What area from the four areas is your strongest personally? Write it below:

2. What is *your group's* weakest area? Write it here:

3. What do you need to do in order to improve yourself and your group in the four areas? Jot down some thoughts here to help you remember what needs to change:

Chapter 18

Three Streams of Small Group Leadership

By Rod

When I graduated from Seminary, I helped plant a church in Gahanna, Ohio. Gahanna is a bedroom community of Columbus, the state capital of Ohio. After we had been in Gahanna several years, someone asked me about our town's name. I didn't know, so I did a little research and found this explanation: "The name *Gahanna* is derived from a Native American word for three creeks joining into one and is the former name of the Big Walnut Creek. The City of Gahanna's Official Seal refers to this confluence of three creeks with the inscription "Three In One."

Imagine that, instead of Gahanna being mistaken for the Biblical *Gehenna* — a burning trash dump outside of Jerusalem that illustrated the eternal torment of hell — it is actually a very respectable Trinitarian illustration. Three streams coming together to form one stream. Not too shabby for a town to be an illustration of the trinity!

Spiritual leadership also has three components that need to come together to form one powerful, moving force. Those three streams need attention and need to be developed in order to become an effective spiritual leader. Here are the three streams:

Biblical

The Bible has some very specific qualities detailed for the official leadership positions in the local church. Those qualities are for Pastors and Deacons and are found in 1 Timothy 3 and Titus 1. The long and short of the official leadership qualities is that a man pretty much should be "blameless." That means that he does not have any major spiritual area that could come into question or attack from the enemy.

Now you may say, "Those scriptures are for pastors, elders and deacons. I'm just a small group leader." Well, the way that most pastors view small group leaders is that they are extensions of the pastoral team that lead the church spiritually. And secondly, why would you not want to strive to be blameless before the Lord? We should all make it our goal to "walk in a manner worthy of the Lord and to please Him in all respects" (Col. 1:10).

Spiritual

2 Corinthians 10 and Ephesians 6 make it clear that the believer is locked in a spiritual conflict against "the power and principalities of this world." The Bible also reveals to us in both passages that we have "weapons" available to us that enable us to become more than conquerors in Christ. Here are just a few weapons available to us as believers and leaders:

- Prayer
- The Word of God
- Spiritual Gifts
- Love
- Righteousness
- Multiplication
- Fasting
- The Spirit of God
- The Church of God
- Sacrifice
- Patience

Many leaders are on the front lines of the battle, but they may not be aware of the weapons and armor that we have as soldiers of the King. Another challenge is that many leaders may be aware of the tools we have at our disposal, but they may not be skilled in using the spiritual arsenal.

Practical

Much has been written in recent years about the conventional competencies of leadership. In fact, many pastors are going to leadership seminars to pick up conventional leader-

Lesson #18: You must be strong in the Biblical, spiritual and practical aspects of small group leadership.

ship tools and habits that they did not get in seminary. Expertise in areas like vision, planning, organization, administration, communication, recruiting, training, and evaluation are helping pastors lead the church. Wise is the small group leader who can receive a vision from God and communicate that clearly to the people entrusted to his or her care. So also are the areas of planning and organization, just to name a few. While it is not necessary that you be an expert in all these areas, you will be a better leader if you practice some of them.

Action Points:

1. Which of the three streams needs the most development in your ministry to your group?

2. Get together with another small group leader from your church and work on a plan for improvement in one of the three areas. If they have not read this chapter, read it together and encourage one another to grow in these areas.

Chapter 19

What Does a Leader Do?
By Rod

Remember when you first learned to ride a bike? Do you remember a few of the instructions? Don't do this . . . make sure you do this . . . and for goodness sake don't ever do that! It was confusing, wasn't it? But once you got started and the wind began to blow in your face, you wanted to ride that bike all the time.

That's the way it is with small group leadership. There are several things to keep in mind and several different skill sets to manage, but once you get the hang of it, leading a group is a lot of fun. To de-mystify the experience of leading a group here are a few important things to keep in mind. The leader must believe in and be committed to:

- Praying at least a half hour a day for self, family, group, church, and the lost.

- Maintaining an outward focus and leading the group toward reaching out to the lost.

- Setting some God-sized goals, then praying and working hard to accomplish them.

- Equipping (training) others to lead his or her

group to create new leaders and prevent personal burnout.

- Determining to successfully launch, multiply, or birth a new group sooner than later.

- Selecting at least one apprentice leader and possibly two. It is important to have a clear cut strategy to eventually birth a new group. If you start your group without an apprentice, it is likely that your group will never plant a new group.

Lesson #19:
Just like riding a bike, once you learn how to lead a small group it's a lot of fun!

- Preparing for the lesson and leads the discussion. Again we will cover this later, but the leader knows where the group is going and how they are going to get there.

- Meeting with his/her coach or pastor on a regular basis and turning in reports as requested. (At least monthly). In a multiplying model, the coach (or pastor acting as the coach) is keeping his or her eyes on some very important vital indicators to see if the group is moving in the right direction.

- Attending all scheduled training and equipping sessions. In order to be effective, leaders need ongoing training and equipping, not to mention the encouragement offered at these events.

- Leading the group in service or ministry projects. The tendency of most groups is that they turn inward and develop an "us four and no more" mentality. Service and ministry projects keep the group focused on others.

- Guiding the group toward reproduction of another group in 12-18 months. The leader keeps an eye on the horizon toward the highest goal of group life, which is healthy spiritual multiplication.

Keeping these multiple priorities in mind and in balance will ensure that you will soon feel the "wind in your face" excitement of leading a healthy, balanced small group.

Action Points:
1. What do you need to do in order to "feel the wind in your face" in your small group? Jot down your thoughts here and share them with your coach or pastor:

2. What do you need to do in order to bring balance to your group or what do you feel is out of balance? Discuss this with your apprentice and/or your coach.

Chapter 20

How Much Prayer?
By Rod

Asking "how much should I pray?" is a little like asking how much oxygen you need to sustain life and function. You don't normally ask that type of question because it is a "given" that you need a lot of oxygen to survive and much more if you are exercising or running a marathon.

The same is true with prayer for the small group leader. The following quotes make a pretty good argument for praying a lot, especially if you are involved in the challenge of fulfilling the Great Commission.

"Prayer must carry on our work as much as preaching; he preacheth not heartily to his people that will not pray for them."   *- Richard Baxter*

"Groanings which cannot be uttered are often prayers which cannot be refused."
                                        - Charles Spurgeon

"Nothing tends more to cement the hearts of Christians than praying together. Never do they love one another so well as when they witness the outpouring of each other's hearts in prayer."
                                        - Charles Finney

"God shapes the world by prayer. The more praying there is in the world the better the world will be, the mightier the forces against evil...."

- E.M.Bounds

"It is possible to move men, through God, by prayer alone." *- Hudson Taylor*

"There has never been a spiritual awakening in any country or locality that did not begin in united prayer." *- D.A.T. Pierson*

"The great people of the earth today are the people who pray, (not) those who talk about prayer...but I mean those who take time and pray." *- S.D.Gordon*

"Work, work, from morning until late at night. In fact, I have so much to do that I shall have to spend the first three hours in prayer." *- Martin Luther*

"All vital praying makes a drain on man's vitality. True intercession is a sacrifice, a bleeding sacrifice." *- J.H. Jowett*

"To get nations back on their feet, we must first get down on our knees." *- Billy Graham*

"Nothing of eternal significance ever happens apart from prayer." *- Jerry Falwell*

"Men may spurn our appeals, reject our message, oppose our arguments, despise our persons, but they are helpless against our prayers."

- *J. Sidlow Baxter*

"History is silent about revivals that did not begin with prayer."

- *Edwin Orr*

Notice the quote by Martin Luther above. His observation was when he found himself really busy, it was the time he prayed more. Not less but more! I was also impacted by the E.M. Bounds' quote where he says, "The more praying there is in the world the better the world will be, the mightier the forces against evil." You can learn a lot from these spiritual giants.

Joel Comiskey has made a study of successful small group leaders. He discovered that groups that multiplied regularly were led by leaders who prayed

**Lesson #20:
A successful
small group leader
is never too busy
to pray.**

an average of an hour a day. In order to do this regularly, you must become intentional, organized, and accountable. Use the action points below to write out what you know you should be praying about, when and where you will pray each day, and with whom you will share this information so they can encourage you.

Action Points:

1. How many minutes each day do you devote to praying for the members and future of your group? Circle one:

      0   5   15   30   60   90+

2. What goal could you set for a daily prayer time? Circle one: 15   30   60   90+

3. Jot down some things you know you need to be praying about concerning your group and its members (so you'll have something specific to pray about each day).

4. When and where will you pray? Deciding this will help you become a prayer warrior.

5. Who can you share with about what you've written here so you can be encouraged to keep praying?

Chapter 21

The Small Group Covenant

By Rod

Zig Ziglar, a Christian motivational speaker, is best known for a famous statement: "If you aim at nothing, you will hit it every time." Here's another quote that I picked up in seminary while attending a homiletics class, "Mist in the pulpit is fog in the pew." Taken together… these statements make one thing clear. Attempting to lead by communicating something that is unclear in your own mind is a bad idea!

All too often, when a small group begins, there is no clear picture of what the leader or the leadership team wants to accomplish. The group may spend several months trying to figure out what they should be attempting to do with their time and talents. The worst case scenario is that the group never develops a clear purpose and never grows and multiplies. For this reason and many others, it is wise to develop a concise and comprehensive group covenant.

Ideally, this information should be covered during the first few meeting times and reviewed periodically. However, if your group has been together for a while and does not have a covenant, you should discuss the need for one in your next meeting. Pray hard your group will agree with you (before you introduce the concept) and then share these basic covenant components as a discussion starter:

1. The Covenant of *Priority*. I will make attendance at and involvement in this group a high priority in my schedule.

2. The Covenant of *Prayer*. I will pray for the members in this group on a regular basis. I will also pray that the Lord of the Harvest will send others to our group.

3. The Covenant of *Outreach*. I believe that our group should reach out and involve others, both believers and those who have yet to believe in Christ as Savior. I will seek to do this to the best of my ability.

4. The Covenant of *Growth*. I will seek personal growth (all areas of my life) and to help the group grow in both quality and quantity.

5. The Covenant of *Openness*. I promise to become an open person; disclosing to you, as well as I am able, my feelings, struggles, joys, and hurts. I will also remain open to involvement in a leadership team for this group or a future group.

6. The Covenant of *Multiplication*. I believe that multiplication is a powerful tool to build the

kingdom of God and will seek to help the leadership team to mature this group to the point where we can multiply or birth another healthy small group.

7. The Covenant of *Availability*. I make available to you—the group and the members—my time, my insight, and my resources.

8. The Covenant of *Confidentiality*. I promise to keep confidential anything shared within the confines of our group, knowing that this is essential to trust and openness between us. I also agree not to share private prayer requests with others unless I have the permission of the person sharing the request.

9. The Covenant of *Accountability*. I recognize that my Christian growth will be enhanced if my walk with Christ and my relationships with others are open to other members of my small group. Therefore, I ask you to watch my life, to check on my progress in achieving my personal and spiritual goals, and to help me become more like Christ.

10. The Covenant of *Love*. I promise to seek to grow in my love for God, for the members of

this group and for people who may not be in this group at this time. I understand love, according to the Parable of the Good Samaritan involves risk, sacrifice, time, and commitment.

When these ten covenant points are covered early and often in a small group, they dramatically increase the clarity and harmony of the group. As the leader, you should make it abundantly clear that your group was formed to minister to one another and reach out, resulting in the birth of new leaders and new groups. In group life, if you don't keep your eyes on the goal of discipleship and growth leading to the birth of a new group, the members begin to believe the group's design is that of exclusivity.

Utilize this newfound information as a springboard for dialog and to move your group into a covenant relationship. Go over this list with your group and challenge them to put each point in their own words to make it unique to your group. While this may be challenging for you, if your group has been together for a season, remember what Yogi Berra said: "If you don't know where you are going, you might not get there." In fact, you may want to begin your group discussion with Yogi's words!

Action Points:

1. Make a note here as to when you will share this covenant with your group and discuss the importance of each point.

   Date _____

2. When you read the sample covenant found in this chapter, ensure your members know that it is just a discussion starter for a truly *customized* covenant relationship and formal covenant. (Your final covenant will certainly look a little different from this generic one.)

3. Communicate with your coach or pastor and let them know what your group has agreed upon so they can support you and pray for you.

Chapter 22

The Importance of
Good Questions

By Rod

Have you ever been in a group that didn't get off to a good start? The leader didn't prepare the study with some good icebreaker questions and as a result, the people in the group never connected relationally. When people don't connect relationally, it makes it more difficult to accomplish the goals of the group. Consider the following questions from the master teacher/leader Himself, Jesus Christ:

- What did you go out in the wilderness to see? A reed shaken in the wind?
- Which is lawful on the Sabbath: to do good or to do evil, to save life or to kill?
- How many hours are there in a day?
- How many loaves do you have?
- Which is easier to say to a paralytic, "Your sins are forgiven, or to say, Get up and walk?"
- Why all this commotion and wailing?
- To a man born blind, "Do you see anything?"
- To His disciples, "Who do men say that I am?"
- To a demon-possessed man, "What is your name?"

- Whose likeness is on this coin?
- What did Moses command?
- To His disciples after the resurrection, "Who are you looking for?"

These questions from the Master were designed to engage His audience and get them thinking about eternal truths. If Jesus was committed to using good questions to introduce His teaching, how much more should we? Good questions, in my experience, come in the form of the "icebreaker" questions before the lesson begins. The purpose is for the people in the group to share about themselves and the set of introductory questions right before the lesson are designed to "hook" the listener's attention. Good questions will open up wonderful avenues of connection and interest. Here are a few icebreaker questions that you may want to use:

Lesson #22: Great icebreaker questions will help your members connect in powerful ways.

- Where did you grow up?
- What was your favorite subject in high school?
- Did you have a nickname in school?
- What is your favorite restaurant? Why?
- If you could go anywhere in the world, where would you go?
- Share three words to describe how you feel right now.

- Describe a typical day in your life in 30 seconds.
- Name one thing that you do well.
- What is the best spiritual advice you ever received?
- Briefly share a time when you believe God led you.
- Can you identify as a spiritual turning point in your life?
- How do you "tune in" to God?
- What is one spiritual goal you are reaching for right now?

Questions like these will enable your group members to learn more about one another, and they will set the stage for group members to receive the "living and active" Word of God. Remember to follow the example of the master teacher and ask good questions throughout the small group experience!

Action Points:

1. Use an icebreaker question in your next meeting that takes the group to the next level in knowing one another. (Remember not to ask too deep of a question or you'll *create* ice, not break it!)

2. Examine the balance of your questions for your next meeting. Can your questions be answered with a "yes" or "no"? If so, rewrite the questions to stir the imagination and to help the members of your group connect to the Word of God.

Chapter 23

Leading Your Small Group Discussion

By Rod

Hebrews 4:12 says, *"For the Word of God is living and active and sharper than any two-edged sword, and piercing as far as the division of soul and spirit, of both joints and marrow, and able to judge the thoughts and intentions of the heart"* (NASB). One of the primary reasons a person comes to a small group is to study and apply the life changing Word of God. Fellowship is fun. Serving people is great. Praying for others and being prayed for is awesome. However, real life change takes place as we come in contact with the living and active Scriptures.

To make sure that you are accurately sharing and applying truths from the Word, you need to make sure that you have some good curriculum (or a good set of questions) and learn how to study your Bible.

This is a very important chapter because you want your group to not only grow in quantity but in *quality*. If you focus on quality, you will gain quantity as a by-product or result. It is vitally important that you are serious about breaking open the bread of life. Here are several suggestions regarding the preparation of a good small group discussion. These suggestions will be especially helpful if your church does not provide you with a weekly agenda to follow based on your pastor's sermon (which is a great way to reinforce and live out what's being taught, and ties your group to the church's weekend services and larger church body).

Curriculum

There are a number of theologically sound publishing ministries that have small group curriculum covering hundreds of Bible passages and topics. Make sure that you choose discussion guides that will move your group past simple or complex Bible study and into life application and ministry to one another (more on this below).

Preparing your own discussion guide

If you are preparing your own outline from scripture, get approval from your pastor or coach. They can help you shape it and improve it, or simply pass it along to other leaders who aren't as skilled as you when it comes to designing a discussion guide.

As you prepare, use these pointers to develop lesson objectives that move it from a boring study to a transformational gathering:

- Determine what you want them to *learn* or gain through the discussion.
- Determine what or how you want them to *feel* after the meeting.
- Determine what you want to *do differently*, *more deeply*, or *start doing* as a group and individuals

through what you've learned and experienced in the meeting.

Once these three objectives have been made clear, you'll do a far better job of creating the right questions based on any scripture you choose.

Icebreakers

Make sure you have some good icebreaker questions at the beginning of your discussion. This is most important when you have first-time visitors

> **Lesson #23: Draw out others with your discussion questions, resisting the urge to do all the talking.**

or when your members are mentally occupied with other things (a deadline at the office or an argument with a family member at dinner before the meeting, just to name a few).

Reading the Bible passage

Always read the passage or verse from the Bible and invite other members to follow along or read a verse or two per person when the passage is long. This will encourage your members to bring their Bibles to your small group and personally read and dig for new truths. It also grounds your discussion.

Observation questions

Good introduction questions that are specific to the passage or outline that you are covering will get people thinking and talking. So ask one or two observation questions about the passage.

Discussion questions

When discussing a passage; ask questions that include:

- What does it say?
- What does it mean?
- How can you apply this to your life?
- Is anything standing in the way of applying it immediately?

Try to have at least one question in the middle of your outline that you can use to go around the room and involve everyone.

Application questions

Create a good set of application questions at the end of the lesson. Make sure that you answer the question, "So what?" for the entire lesson. By the time a person leaves the group for that time period, he or she should be challenged to put something specific into practice.

General Guidelines

- Avoid lecturing (or doing all the talking) even if you have to bite your tongue to keep quiet and just ask the questions. The Word of God is powerful. If you challenge your members to read it as a group, ask open-ended questions which have several possible answers, and then make personal application, your members will find opportunities to confess sin, share deeply, and apply what is being discussed.

- Determine what you are hoping to accomplish with the discussion. Some leaders find it helpful to keep a journal of what they were hoping to accomplish in meetings and if it happened or not. A simple journal is a great way to keep track of your expectations and gives you solid information to discuss with your coach or pastor when asked how your meetings are going.
- Don't let the discussion get off track. Keeping your goals in mind will help you remember this. (I'll discuss how to handle "difficult people" in another chapter.)

If you keep these basics in mind, then God's Word—the "two-edged sword" —will have a powerful effect on the members of your group. Remember, quality will always produce quantity.

Action Points:

1. Which of these basic discussion issues is your weakest? Write it here:

2. Compose several good questions that you can use in any small group context. Write them in your Bible so you'll always have them ready if necessary.

Chapter 24

How to Find and Train
an Apprentice

By Rod

When asked the question, "How do you train a person?" Albert Schweitzer answered, "There are three ways to train a person … the first is by example. The second is by example and the third is by example." This type of clarity is echoed in the New Testament when the Apostle Paul said these words:

"Whatever you have learned or received or heard from me, or seen in me—put it into practice. And the God of peace will be with you." (Php. 4:9)

"Follow my example, as I follow the example of Christ." (1 Cor. 11:1)

"Join with others in following my example, brothers, and take note of those who live according to the pattern we gave you." (Php. 3:17)

In these scriptures, Paul was saying, "Christianity is more caught than taught!" The same is true for training an apprentice. The way to train someone to lead a group is "up close and personal." This is not an academic endeavor from some book. This is discipling another with "life on life" mentorship.

Through the centuries, trades were primarily taught through close supervision and mentorship. As the person progressed, the master would entrust more and more responsibility to the apprentice until he or she was ready to take on the full weight of the responsibility. Training a small group leader is no different. Here are some good suggestions to train an apprentice to lead a small group:

1. Pray that God would send and reveal your apprentice.

2. Look for someone in your group who is eager to serve and friendly.

3. Look for someone who has F.A.I.T.H., which stands for:

   Faithful
   Available (for the tasks ahead)
   Integrity (a person with character)
   Teachable
   Heart for God

4. Before you ask him or her to apprentice under you, give the person some responsibilities every week to see if they take the ball and run with it:

   • Ice Breaker   • Introduction to the Lesson
   • Prayer Time   • Outreach Projects

5. After you have watched him or her for a couple of weeks, talk to your coach or pastor. He or she may have concerns, or will want to know that you are pursuing the potential leader for a future leadership position in the small group ministry.

6. If you and your coach (or pastor) pray about the invitation and decide the person is a good fit for leadership in your group and the timing is right, approach the person together. Encourage the person by what you have already seen. Explain the process of apprenticeship, which carries a short-term goal of leading a new group or taking over your existing group.

> **Lesson #24:**
> **Raising up others to lead a small group effectively is a result of your example and mentorship.**

7. When he or she accepts the call of leadership, meet with him or her before the group meets to pray and review the goals for the evening and then briefly afterward to discuss what you both observed and experienced.

8. As soon as possible, ask your new apprentice to lead one discussion per month to "learn by doing" and contact various members to pray for them and encourage them. Everyone learns by experiencing some struggle or failure, so antici-

pate this and praise your apprentice for his or her hard work regardless of the outcome.

9. From this point on, take your apprentice with you to leadership events and meetings with your coach or pastor (unless told otherwise by your leadership). You may also want to accompany your apprentice to your church's small group leader training events. This shows support and you can help him or her follow through and practice what is being learned in each session.

10. Evaluate the person's progress when you meet with your coach or pastor. Note specific things that need attention and talk with your coach or pastor about the best way to move the person closer to being a strong small group leader.

11. Help your apprentice start a new group or take over your group so you can start a new group. The healthiest new small groups have a leader, an apprentice, a worship leader, and a host. Insure the new group has this before they start or take over your group.

12. Visit with the new leader regularly to see how his or her group is doing. Your relationship does not end when you are both leading groups! The new leader needs your friendship and prayer support throughout his or her ministry as a leader.

Using a comprehensive 12-point checklist like this can get you started down the path of effectively developing and mentoring others for small group leadership. Mentoring others will enable you to experience the joy that comes from helping babes in Christ become warriors for Christ!

Action Points:

1. Who has F.A.I.T.H. in your group and could be approached to lead a part of an upcoming meeting or serve another member of the group?

2. What can you ask them to do, and when will you ask?

3. If you already have an apprentice, it's time to help them find their own apprentice and start the process again. Discuss this with him or her as soon as possible.

Chapter 25

Birthing a New Group
By Rod

Those who have firsthand experience have told me that giving birth is painful. I have also been told by every mother who has ever birthed a child that it was worth all the pain to bring that baby into the world. Just think of the juxtaposition of the pain of childbirth and the joy that the baby brings to the parents. In the physical world of birthing children, there is no joy without pain. This seems to be the case when it comes to starting or birthing new groups as well.

People in small groups often feel an emotional uneasiness as leadership discusses birthing a new group. The motivation for starting new groups is simple. The world is growing at an exponential rate and any system or structure that is not based upon an exponential strategy is destined to fail. That is why we must design and develop disciples and churches that multiply!

However, small group multiplication goes against the grain of most people's desire to keep their fellowship intact. I call this the "us four and no more" factor. Most people don't mind getting involved in a group and adding new members to the group, but if you ask them to birth a new group … what they hear from you sounds like:

"perform a 'c-section' on yourself without the benefit of anesthesia."

So what can be done to overcome this enormous challenge? I believe you need to focus on three things:

The Harvest

In John 4:35 Jesus says, *"Do you not say, 'Four months more and then the harvest'? I tell you, open your eyes and look at the fields! They are ripe for harvest."* In your community there are multitudes that have never heard the gospel of Christ. Yet we are content to minister to each other while the "ninety and nine" are "distressed and down cast like sheep without a shepherd." One of our most difficult challenges as Great Commission leaders is to keep the focus on the lost in a disciple making structure. Helping people to lift up their eyes (off themselves) and to focus on others is a challenge, but it is a worthwhile goal.

Prayer

Joel Comiskey has studied groups that multiplied and the common denominator is this one element: the leaders prayed on average an hour a day. Jesus asked a rhetorical question of His disciples in the Garden of Gethsemane, "Could you not watch with me for one hour?" I believe that multiplication in the spiritual world is no different than multiplication in the material world. Multiplication is always the result of intimacy. As we spend time with God we develop His heart, His eyes, and His desire to reach out to the lost and hurting. If we are not spending time with God we will not develop His passion or His principles for reaching the world, which is multiplication.

Making Disciples and Developing Leaders

Jesus said when a "disciple is fully trained; he will be like his Master." Sometimes I ask a question in the classes that I teach at Liberty Theological Seminary, "How many of you want to be like Jesus?" Everyone who is paying attention raises his or her hand.

Then I ask, "Was Jesus a leader?" The answer of course, is yes. Jesus was a leader, but His leadership led to reaching people with the gospel and then helping them grow to the point where they also participated in the Great Commission (making disciples). When a disciple is fully trained, he or she will be involved somehow and somewhere in the process of making disciples who develop into leaders who make disciples. In a group setting this is difficult, but if you keep the focus on the harvest fields and on intimacy with God and on developing disciples who produce leaders, it will become a reality.

> **Lesson #25:**
> **Birthing a new group group requires vision and a lot of prayer.**

A basic definition of leadership is simply stated as "influence." Great Commission leaders must be influencing those "allotted to your charge" to become multiplying leaders (patting your head) who will at the same time develop a multiplying strategy to reach the world for Christ (rubbing your stomach). The ultimate goal is to stand before Christ and hear from Him, "well done, good and faithful servant!"

Action Points:

1. Are you praying daily for a harvest of new believers and new leaders through your own life and in your group? Make it the first thing you pray about every day for the next 21 days to develop a new habit.

2. In your next small group meeting, read John 4:35 and lead your group in a time of prayer. Ask each member to specifically ask God to reveal those who are dying to know Him because they are all around you.

Chapter 26

How to Develop a Good Host for Your Group

By Rod

The natural division of responsibilities in a small group environment seems to be along these lines: Small Group Leader, Small Group Apprentice, Small Group Worship Leader, and Small Group Host. The Small Group Host has the important ministry of hospitality. He or she accomplishes this ministry by thinking about the needs of the members and visitors who gather together for a meeting. It is the host's responsibility to eliminate distractions that could hinder a person from being able to focus on spiritual matters. Hosts are also likely to be the first people with whom newcomers come in contact, so they have a tremendous opportunity to initiate an atmosphere of love and acceptance to all who walk through their doors. The host's role, then, is to make sure people feel completely welcomed and wanted. Hosting a small group is an honor, and it must be done with a commitment to excellence.

With that in mind, consider the following guidelines for hosting a small group. It is important that hosts remain sensitive to the following issues and are able to create an environment that would be conducive for a good meeting.

The meeting place

Make sure that the meeting room is tidy, pleasant, free of strong odors, and enough chairs (including at least one extra chair) have been brought into the room where the group will meet and arranged in a circle. Also, make sure that the bathroom is clean and supplied with soap and toilet paper. While it's not a requirement, the host should provide water, tea, or coffee for those who have arrived.

Be prepared

The first task of a host is to greet people when they come to the door and take their coat if it's wintertime. Newcomers are often the first to arrive. Their first impression of a group is critical. An excellent host will be ready and relaxed in advance of the starting time to greet people. A warm greeting and an encouraging word from the host as people show up sets the tone for the whole evening.

Encourage the host to strike up a conversation with those who are quiet or new to the group. Asking the person where they live, how they heard about the small group, and about their family (spouse, kids, parents) are a few good examples of introductory questions.

Next, be sure you are well supplied for anything you may need for your meeting by arriving early and visiting with the host about the evening's events. Be sure you have plenty of pencils, paper, Bibles, study guides, song sheets, tissue, and anything else the members will need for the meeting.

Finally, pay attention to the details that follow in the next points. These may seem a bit trivial, but careful attention to them will display an extra concern for your group members.

Lighting and audio/visuals

Ask the host to adjust the lighting if necessary. Be sure the room where the small group is held is well lit. Also, meet in a circle where everyone can see each other's faces to facilitate equal participation and sharing. If your group is using a DVD as a discussion starter, the equipment should be set up in advance and "cued" so there's no fiddling with discs, remote controls, or wires during the meeting.

The thermostat

Ask the host to keep an eye on the room temperature and adjust the thermostat accordingly. A room that is too cold will make it very difficult for

> **Lesson #26:**
> **Eliminate assumptions.**
> **Help your group's host create a warm environment for ministry to take place.**

people to remain comfortable in their chairs for any length of time and they will be be less likely to fellowship. A room that is too hot will cause people to become drowsy. The more people you have in a room, the warmer it will become, so consider the temperature during the meeting as well. One expert suggests 67 degrees as an ideal room temperature for groups. If the room is stuffy, ask the host to turn on a fan to draw fresh air into the room or open a window.

Eliminate distractions

Ask the host to put dogs, cats, and noisy birds in a separate room or outside for the evening. Let the answering machine pick up the host's calls and turn off the ringer and the speaker so the phone does not interrupt the meeting. (If you've ever been in a small group meeting where the whole group stopped to listen to the caller leave a message you know what I'm talking about.) If the host is playing soft music as people arrive—which is a great idea, by the way—ask them to turn it off before you formally begin your meeting.

Snacks

Food is a great catalyst for building community. Ask your group's host to create a sign-up sheet so the group can enjoy a light snack or dessert following your meeting. Guard your host from buying and preparing the snacks for the group every week. Adding the financial and time aspects of preparing snacks for the group each week will burn out a wonderful host quickly.

All of these points are important to provide a suitable place for your small group to meet. Instead of having one host home, you can also take turns hosting the group. This provides an excellent opportunity to get to know all the members in your group in a more personal way. This also gives the member a perfect opportunity to invite unchurched friends who may not feel comfortable going into a stranger's home.

Action Points:

1. Quickly glance over the areas in this article and note any of the hosting issues that need attention in your next meeting. Then, ask your host if you can arrive 20-30 minutes early when you next meet. When you arrive, ask them to re-read this chapter with you to review the basics.

2. At your next meeting, ask the members of the group if you can meet in their home. For any member who opens their home in the future, you'll need to visit with them beforehand and read this chapter together to insure the home is ready for your small group meeting.

Chapter 27

Eight Habits of Effective Small Group Leaders

By Dave

Why do some small groups grow and multiply, while others go nowhere? Is there some activity or a set of activities a small group leader can do to increase the probability of his or her group growing and multiplying? If so, are these activities beyond the reach of the average small group leader and will it take years of training to master them? Or is there a set of activities that are simple, attainable, and realistic enough that any small group leader who wants to grow and multiply can put them into their weekly schedule?

I have had the privilege of leading small groups and coaching small group leaders for over thirty years. It began as a 16-year-old public school student when my friend and I started lunchtime Bible studies at our high school. These groups "accidentally" grew and multiplied. In college, I started a discipleship group that spread over the campus. During my summer mission trips while in college I got to start groups in little towns in England and in high rises on Manhattan in New York City. When I graduated, I started groups in rural Virginia. Then I was hired to train, write curriculum, and oversee 300 small group leaders at a large Christian university. Later, I started a group in my basement that grew into a church with over a hundred groups.

Some of these various groups grew and multiplied, and some did not. Through the years I noticed that the long-range effectiveness of a leader and a group revolved around some simple habits that were practiced outside the group meeting.

Lesson #27: Following these eight habits will help your group grow and multiply.

Several years ago I wanted to help the leaders I was coaching know exactly what it would take for them to be more effective. By studying small group ministry and thinking through my own experience, I identified eight regular practices that seemed to make the difference between effectiveness and ineffectiveness. I put them into a simple list of eight habits that would enhance the effectiveness of a small group leader. They are as follows:

1. Dream of leading a healthy, growing, multiplying group.
2. Pray for your group members daily.
3. Invite new people to visit your group weekly.
4. Contact your group members regularly.
5. Prepare for your group meeting.
6. Mentor an apprentice leader.
7. Plan group fellowship activities.
8. Be committed to your own personal growth.

I began by asking the leaders I coached to adopt these habits and build them into their weekly schedules. Without exception, those who did these habits become highly effective leaders who grew and multiplied their groups. (By the way, those who did not adopt the habits did not multiply their groups.) What was especially interesting was that gifts, personality, and experience were not as important as the commitment to the eight habits. Leaders who did not have the gift of teaching or who had not been Christians for a long time, but followed the eight habits became effective. Those leaders who were more introverted or had never led before and practiced the habits were growing and multiplying their group. Practicing these eight habits — not their personalities or gifts — caused their groups to grow.

After teaching these habits for several years I have come to several conclusions:

✓ The eight habits really do work.
✓ The eight habits are universal in nature.
✓ The eight habits have broad application.
✓ These habits are easy to understand and remember.
✓ The best quality about these habits is that they are "doable" or realistic.
✓ The eight habits are motivating.
✓ The eight habits are challenging, but not overwhelming.

The eight habits can take you and those serving alongside you to a new level. Whether you are an apprentice, a novice small group leader, a seasoned leader, a coach of small group leaders, a director of a district of groups, or the pastor of a large small groups ministry, the eight habits will work for you. These habits are a path that leads to fruitfulness and multiplication, helping leaders, and those under them, experience greater fulfillment in ministry.

In the next several chapters I will discuss these eight habits. You will learn what they are, why they are important, and most importantly, how to apply them.

Action Point:

1. Consider your existing leadership disciplines in your small group. How do they compare with the eight habits overviewed in this chapter? How many are you already doing? List them here.

[This chapter is adapted in part from the introduction of the book, *Eight Habits of Effective Small Group Leaders* by Dave Earley, (Houston, TX: Touch Publications, 2001)]

Chapter 28

It Starts With a Dream
By Dave

Two couples received the same training as small group leaders. Brian and Susan began a new group with the dream of ministering to young parents in a healthy, growing, multiplying group.

Mark and Kathy took over an existing group. Primarily, they did this because their pastor asked them to do it. They did not have their own dream for the group, and viewed leading the group as a favor for the church. For the first six months, both couples worked hard inviting and contacting people, but both groups stayed small.

Mark and Kathy were discouraged. They soon lost what little dream their pastor had for their group and began to go through the motions of group leadership. They stopped praying for their people or contacting them regularly. They quit inviting new folks. They did not take much time to prepare for the meetings. They did not create any fellowship activities. Now the dream was gone. As a result, their small group kept shrinking and within a year it died. Discouraged, they left the church.

Brian and Susan did not lose sight of their dream. Eventually their efforts started to pay off. Within a year, their group had taken off and they quickly ran out of room. Their group continued to grow and eventually multiplied. The dream made the difference.

Most small groups and small group leaders are sleeping giants. Satan wants to keep them that way, so he constantly whispers lies to small group leaders about what they *can't* do. Satan is defeated when small group leaders get a dream of what they and their group can become. Possessing a big dream for your group increases your potential to make a difference for God's kingdom.

Effective small groups have staggering potential. The Methodist church movement traces its beginning to a small accountability group at Oxford University. Today it has 11 million members!

Effective groups are the untapped potential of the local church. Not only can they multiply to reach large numbers of people, they can be spiritual hospitals for the hurting and hothouses for spiritual growth. They are hands and feet for the heart of Jesus. They can be the breeding ground for leaders and the launching pad for spiritual warfare. They give people a feeling of belonging. Effective small groups create teams for evangelism. Yet all of this potential often goes unrealized without a dream.

**Lesson #28:
Great small groups are the result of big dreams.**

God wants to raise up an army of strong small group leaders who will grow and multiply groups in such a way as to shake this world. He wants to awaken the sleeping giants.

Someone observed that the potential of a man is measured by the goals he pursues. Few people realize even a fraction of their potential. Having a dream helps a small group leader begin to realize their awesome potential to make a difference for God.

Dream of leading a healthy, growing, multiplying group. Envision leading your group to multiply every year. Believe God can use your small group to make a big difference.

Having a dream puts everything into perspective. Even tasks that are difficult, mundane, or unrewarding take on added value when you know they will ultimately contribute to the fulfillment of your dream.

Being an effective small group leader is more than just leading a group. It is raising up leaders in order to reach the world. It is facilitating the body of Christ to minister to its members. It is creating a spiritual family and building a spiritual army. When small group leaders understand this dream, they immediately raise the value of their group and each of its members.

Action Points:

1. What is your dream for your group? Write it below. (If you don't have a clear dream and a definite date for multiplication, you should fast and pray until God gives you a definite picture of what He wants your group to be and do for Him.)

2. As you formulate or clarify your dream, tell your coach or pastor about the dream and ask them to pray with you concerning the fulfillment of the dream. They are on your side and want you to succeed.

[This chapter is adapted from chapter one of the book, *Eight Habits of Effective Small Group Leaders* by Dave Earley, Houston TX: Touch Publications, 2001.]

Chapter 29

The Power of Prayer

By Dave

Many years ago, evangelist S. D. Gordon said, "The greatest thing anyone can do for God and man is to pray."[1] Prayer is the most important activity for a small group leader. To put it a different way, if you only did one thing to make your group more effective, that one thing would be to pray.

Prayer is the one of the simplest things you can do as well. At any time of day, in any place you find yourself, you can advance your group and minister to your group members through prayer. Yet, most small group leaders would admit that prayer is the hardest thing to do consistently. They're busy. They're distracted. They're discouraged … and just do not pray enough.

Highly effective small group leaders view prayer as an indispensable tool in their ministry to others. They use it often and well. They build it into their daily schedule and make it a high priority. They don't just pray a little, they pray a *lot*.

Prayer is "job one"

As mentioned in chapter 20, a survey of small group leaders revealed an interesting correlation between time spent in prayer and small group multiplication. It revealed that leaders who spent *90 minutes or more* in daily devotions multiplied their groups *twice as often* as those who spent less than half an hour.[2] Never underestimate the power of prayer!

Winning the fight to make time to pray will make success in the other habits much easier. Failure here will make success with the other habits nearly impossible.

Prayer is a powerful time-saving device

How many times have you and I said, "I am so busy" or "I just don't seem to have enough time to pray?" Such statements reveal a misunderstanding about the nature of prayer. Prayer actually saves time and effort. Prayer allows God to do things in short periods of time that you could not accomplish without Him in months or even years of work.

How often have you taught, encouraged, counseled, and rebuked people with little or no result? How often have you shared your faith with seemingly little or no breakthrough in the other person's defenses? But, when God moves, He helps people make changes in seconds, where you could not get them to do it in years. Prayer is a powerful time saver. Once you understand this you will learn to say, "I am too busy *not* to pray."

> Lesson #29:
> Prayer is powerful and changes everything.

Prayer invites God to work

You can't meet with all of your small group members twenty-four hours a day, but God can. You can't go with all of your small group members to their homes or with them to work, but God can. You can't be at two or more places at once, but God can!

Prayer brings God into the situation; nothing is too hard for God (Jeremiah 32:17). He does great things as a result of prayer.

Prayer has no regrets

No one ever comes to the end of their life saying, "I prayed too much." But many come to the end of their lives saying, "I prayed too little." Likewise, no small group leader has ever looked back and said, "I think I spent too much time praying for our group this week." But far too many look back and say, "I think I spent too little time praying for my group."

Prayer is our greatest spiritual weapon

As a small group leader, you must pray consistently to keep from being defeated by Satan's persistent attacks on you, your family, and your group. To fail to pray is to fail altogether. Satan will not let you easily plunder his kingdom because when you rob his kingdom of lost souls, he can't get them back! He will not passively allow you to grow and multiply, evangelize, and equip. He is fighting you every inch of the way.

We must not only pray to keep from losing ground, but also pray in order to take ground. On our own, we are not more powerful than the enemy, but we are when we pray. We can fight him successfully and march forward on our knees. Only one weapon will hold him off and push him back. It is the weapon of prayer. This is why we must pray without ceasing.

Action Point:

Schedule time (or times) to spend with God in prayer every day of the week. Remember to take some of your time to be silent and listen to what He might tell you about the dream for your group.

Notes
1. S.D. Gordon, *Quiet Talks on Prayer*, (New York, NY, Grosset and Dunlap, 1941), p. 12.
2. Joel Comiskey, *Home Group Cell Explosion* (Houston, TX, TOUCH Publications. 1998), p. 34.

[This chapter is adapted from chapter two of the book, *Eight Habits of Effective Small Group Leaders* by Dave Earley, (Houston TX: TOUCH Publications, 2001)]

Chapter 30

If You Invite Them, They Will Come

By Dave

For several years, our family led a group of high school students. We saw dozens of unchurched kids come to Christ. About half of them have become regular church-goers, and many of those brought their parents to church. We did several things to attract and win so many seekers, but the single biggest factor was simply inviting them to our parties, events, and small group meetings.

When it comes to inviting, we followed one simple principle: *If you invite them, they will come.* Occasionally I have heard small group leaders say that they do not invite people "because they might not come." When people tell me this, I always ask, "If you invite them, what is the worse thing that could happen?" They generally respond, "They might not come."

Then I reply, "If they are not coming anyway, have you lost anything? After all, they just *might* come if you invite them, right?" It is exciting to know that if you invite them, they will come. Not all will come. Not all will come right away, but if you invite them, *some* will come.

According to Richard Price and Pat Springer,

> Experienced group leaders . . . realize that you usually have to personally invite 25 people for 15 to say they will attend. Of those 15, usually only eight to 10 will actually show up, and of those, only five to seven will be regular attendees after a month or so.[1]

This means you can grow a new group of ten to fourteen regular members in a year by inviting one new person each week! If a whole group catches the vision of inviting, a group can experience explosive growth. When I start a new group, I start by asking two to five times the number of people I expect at the first meeting.

Where do I find people to invite?

There are at least four good places to look for people to invite:
- Family members who live in your town.
- Friends who live nearby.
- Coworkers or fellow students.
- Neighbors who live on your street.

Tips for Effective Inviting

Saturate the situation in prayer

God knows the "what, when, where, and how" of an effective invitation. Prayer helps us to cooperate with what He is doing. Saturating the invitation with prayer before you ask the person will help you hear God on issues of timing and what to invite them to (a barbeque at your home with other group members, your small group meeting, or an Easter service, for example). Each day, petition God for His heart for the person you'd like to invite and you'll soon discover a newfound confidence when it's time to ask.

Keep them saying "Yes"

Once someone has said "No" to an invitation, it can be easier for them to say "No" to the next invitation, so it is valuable to get them to say "Yes" and to keep them saying "Yes." If possible, build a bridge of "Yeses" until they are regular attendees of your group.

For example, some people invite a person to a group before the person is ready to say "Yes" to a group. However, the person may be ready to say "Yes" to allowing their children to attend a chil-

> Lesson #30:
> Effective leaders consistently invite new people to attend their group.

dren's activity at the church or "Yes" to going to a ball game with you and a few of your small group members.

Obviously, different people have different progressions of "Yes." Pray about finding the thing they will say "Yes" to, and start from that point.

Perseverance

Too often, we invite people once, they say

"No," and we give up. And quite frequently, we invite them to come and they say "Yes," but do not show, so we do not invite them again. Don't give up on a person too easily and quit inviting too quickly! Persistence makes a difference. I find that many people who do not come at the first invitation often come after the third or fourth, *if* I have continued to build a caring relationship.

Team inviting

Inviting is easiest when inviting is done in concert with a team of people, a posse of prayer, and a healthy group and church. You do not have to do it all by yourself. It is especially powerful when the person you are trying to reach already knows and likes someone else in your church or small group. So, build relational bridges between the people you want to invite to your group and other members of your group. I've already shared some ideas as to how to do this, so consider the fun things your group is doing in the future and how you can involve your unchurched friends and family.

Capitalizing on the seasons of the soul

People have seasons when they are more open to the Gospel. Most adults come to Christ, or come back to Christ, out of one of these seasons:

- Death of a loved one
- Divorce
- Marriage
- Family problems
- Major illness
- Birth of a child
- Move to a new neighborhood, city, job, or school

The wise leader is sensitive to these seasons. Lovingly use them to increase ministry to the person you hope to invite. If at all possible, involve other members of your group. These seasons of life give your group members a great opportunity to reach out and serve your unchurched friend by doing yard work, helping them move into their new apartment, making a meal and bringing it to their home, or making them feel comfortable in a new town where they have very few friends.

Inviting people to get to know other members of your group and to your small group meetings is a habit you cannot afford to neglect out of fear of rejection. You have nothing to lose if they say "No." However, they have everything to lose, so be bold and start inviting people into your small group relationships! Remember, if you invite them, they will come.

Action Points:

1. Make a list of local family members, friends, coworkers or fellow students, and neighbors who are unchurched.

2. Share this list with your group next week and ask them to pray with you about inviting each of them to a group event like a barbeque or a small group meeting.

3. Start inviting these people, and encourage your group to hold you accountable each week for how many invitations you extended. This will model a lifestyle of invitation for them and you can then ask them to start inviting as well.

Notes
1. Price and Springer, *Rapha's Handbook for Group Leaders* (Houston, TX: Rapha Publishing, 1991), p. 132.

[This chapter is adapted from chapter three of the book, *Eight Habits of Effective Small Group Leaders*, by Dave Earley, (Houston TX: TOUCH Publications, 2001)]

Chapter 31

How to Fill Your Empty Chair
By Dave

Years ago I attended a leadership seminar where the instructor presented a session called, "Problems Every Small Group Leader Will Have." When asked about how to help a group continue to reach out and grow, he described the principle of the Empty Chair with this statement: "At every meeting, an empty chair is pulled into the circle and the group is asked to pray for someone to fill the chair at the next meeting."[1]

Of course, every growing group does not use a literal empty chair, although many do. The principle remains: growing groups remain perpetually vigilant of the need to reach out to unchurched people.

Five Fields of People to Invite to Your Group:

Family
Ministry flows best through the channel of relationships. Think about it. Moses led Israel with the help of his brother Aaron (Exodus 4:14-15), Peter met Jesus through the invitation of his brother

Andrew (Jn. 1:40-42), and John followed Jesus
alongside of his brother James (Mk. 1:17-21). Even
though they were very skeptical of Jesus when He
launched His ministry, eventually His family came
around. His younger brother, James, became the
leader of the Jerusalem church (Matt. 4:21; Acts
12:17; 15:13-29; 21:17-19; 1 Cor. 15:7) and the
author of a book of the Bible bearing his name.
Jude, another younger brother, also penned a book
of the Bible.

Do you have brothers or sisters, aunts and
uncles, cousins, nieces or nephews within driving
distance of your group? You already have a blood
connection and at least some history with them.
These are the first people you should invite.

Friends

Friends should be the easiest and most natural connection for you to invite to your group. You have already won them to yourself. You and your friend know a lot about each other. They have seen the genuine "you." If Jesus is real in your life, He longs to attract them to Himself through you. Invite your friends to your group.

Coworkers or fellow students

God did not place you in your job or in that school by accident. There are people there He knew would be receptive to you. The people you see everyday are a fertile field for ministry. Get to know them as unique individuals and take them out of the landscape of your life. Listen to their hurts and hang-ups, truly befriending them. Then, when you invite them to your group, they'll come.

> **Lesson #31: Invite people to your group from within your web of relationships.**

Neighbors

Make a point of getting to know your neighbors to see who is looking for God. Be the one on your street who is always going out of your way to strike up a conversation and serve them. Take them baked treats or an extra bag of fruit when you get a great deal at the market. Invite them over for dessert. Much like your job or school, you are

God's representative on your block as well. Get to know your neighbors, and serve them when they have needs, creating friendships. As you learn about their background and struggles and deepen your relationship, invite them to your group.

Church contacts

Often the most obvious and neglected place to look for new group members is within your church. Become aware of those church members who are currently unconnected to a group. Get to know first-time guests to your worship services, and invite them to lunch after church. Introduce them to other members of your group before and after your services, and extend an invitation to visit your group. If they weren't interested in new relationships with Christians, they wouldn't be visiting your services.

If you approach each day with your eyes open to the possibilities, you will be absolutely amazed at the number of people God will bring across your path or into your sphere of influence that you can get to know and invite to your group. Learn to take advantage of every opportunity to build those redemptive relationships.

Action Points:

1. Take time each day this week to pray and ask God what area of your life is filled with opportunities to invite others to your small group. Is it among the parents of your children's friends? How about the person in the cubicle next to you who was just transferred into your part of the company from out of town? What about family, friends, or neighbors?

2. As God reveals this to you, don't be timid. Ask them to come to your next meeting, or to a group-sponsored event like a barbeque. When you invite them, tell them you're happy to pick them up and bring them along. Remember, if you don't ask, they probably won't come!

Notes
1. Lyman Coleman, *Small Group Training Manual*, (Littleton, CO., Serendipity House, 1991), p. 79.
2. Dave Earley, *Eight Habits of Effective Small Group Leaders*, (Houston TX, TOUCH Publications, 2001), p. 40.

Chapter 32

If You Continue to Contact Them, They Will Continue to Come

By Dave

We started New Life Church in my basement with 11 adults. The church grew to 100 people worshipping each week in six months and to over 200 in 18 months. During those first 18 months, I called almost every family every week. I spend a few evenings a week and Saturday afternoon making five-minute phone calls until the church got to an average attendance over 200. Then the five members of our leadership team divided the calling between us. We found that the principle of contacting was huge for us, and it's no different for your small group.

Contacting helps your group grow

After the first visit to your small group, the highly effective small group leader will contact the visitor. This usually involves a short phone call thanking them for coming, asking how they liked the group, and inviting them to return. This is the beginning of your relational connection to the person, and can easily turn them into an active member if you keep calling them each week.

My sons held evangelistic Bible studies in their public middle school. The group met each Wednesday morning 45 minutes before school. Within a couple of months, they had grown the group to 25 kids, most of whom were unchurched.

How did they do it? On Tuesdays, they would invite kids at school. On Tuesday evenings, they were on the phone making short phone calls or sending messages from their computers. They found that the principle of contacting works. If they contacted their friends, they came. On some Tuesday nights, they had extra homework or were busy with friends and forgot to contact. When this happened, the attendance fell off dramatically.

> **Lesson #32:**
> **Effective group leaders keep in regular contact with group members outside of the meeting time.**

Your adult or family group will be no different. If you make a short phone call to each visitor who comes to your group, they are far more likely to come back.

Contacting increases your average weekly attendance

Someone asked me, "Is it really that important for everyone to be there?" My answer was, "If it is not worth encouraging them to attend, why are you leading a group?" I think our church services and small group meetings are worth attending. A person will benefit more by being there than they would by not being there. Therefore, I contact them to increase attendance.

Contacting your small group members regularly will increase the number of times they attend in a year because it provides a friendly accountability. More frequent participation in your small group meetings increases the number of times God can work in and through their lives, giving them a clear spiritual purpose in life.

If you've noticed that some of your members are "hit and miss" with small group meeting attendance, start calling them each week and watch their attendance become far more consistent. After you've developed a good habit of calling a few of your members, call the balance and watch your group grow.

Contacting helps a shepherd know the state of his or her flock

The better you know your members, the better you will lead them. Or, to put it another way, "you can't grow them if you don't know them."

Someone in your small group may be going through a situation that they are reluctant to share with the group, but they will share it with you when you contact them. It is amazing what people will tell you when you make contact with them over the phone, in person, or by e-mail. Use regular contacts to get to know your members outside of meetings and they'll open up to you. (One of the biggest mistakes leaders make in selecting apprentices is failing to know them well enough.

See the suggestions given later in this chapter for how to learn your people's heart through contacting.)

Contacting communicates that you care

Contacting your members communicates that you says care enough about the person to sacrifice some free time to make the contact. Contacting them also says that you care enough about them to find out why they were absent or what they think of the group.

People drop out of groups because they do not feel nurtured. Contacting them regularly and asking about prayer requests shared in and out of the group, how they are doing, and what they might contribute to the group is powerful.

Suggestions that Make Contacting Powerful

1. Ask them, "How may I pray for you?"

2. Ask them, "What do you want God to do about this?" or "What does God want you to do about this?"

3. Say, "Let's pray right now." Then pray for them right then, aloud.

4. Then ask, "Do you want to pray?"

Suggestions for what to talk about as part of regular contact

1. Is there anything special in your life going on this week?

2. How are your kids doing?

3. Do you like your job?

4. On a scale of one to ten, how stressful was your week?

5. Where did you grow up?

6. How were you saved?

7. When were you baptized?

8. What do you like most about our church?

9. What do you like best about our small group?

10. What area do you think God wants you to grow in this month?

11. What are the things everyone says you do really well?

12. Have you ever thought of leading a group?

Action Points:

1. Put the names and phone numbers of all your members in your cell phone or on a single sheet of paper so you can easily call each person.

2. Call each member on your list and use the questions in this chapter as a springboard to get to know them better. A five-minute call is long enough.

3. When you call, remember to get them talking and then focus on listening, not doing all the talking yourself. The goal is to get to know them and help them know you care by actively listening to what they have to say to you.

[This chapter is adapted from chapter four of the book, *Eight Habits of Effective Small Group Leaders* by Dave Earley, (Houston TX: Touch Publications, 2001.)]

Chapter 33

Preparation is the Foundation of Success

By Dave

"Failing to prepare is preparing to fail."
John Wooden, Hall of Fame basketball coach

"Preparation is not my strong suit," Bill explains. Bill usually "flies by the seat of his pants" when it comes to facilitating his group meetings. He says that he likes his group to be "free and spontaneous."

But lately, attendance has dropped off. No one has invited any guests in a while. The people in his group are grumbling, saying the group has turned into a time where "Bill just shares his pet peeves."

On the other hand, Dan and his apprentice, Doug, spend time on Monday nights getting ready for their Tuesday night group meeting. The time they spend praying and preparing makes the small group meeting successful. Their group has grown. The group members look forward to coming every week and are not ashamed to invite guests. Dan and Doug have learned that a successful small group meeting does not fall together haphazardly. It is the product of planning, prayer, and preparation.

The highly effective small group leader

develops a habit of preparing for the group meeting. He or she carves out the time and puts in the effort to be ready for "the most important hour and a half of the week" for each person in the group. The effective leader know that the beginning of leadership is "knowing where you are going." Weekly preparation keeps a group moving upward and onward for God.

I want to encourage you to spend at least as long preparing for your group as your group will last. That means if your group lasts an hour and a half, spend at least that long preparing for it beforehand, if not twice as long. It will be worth it.

Wise leaders have found when they are prepared, God has greater opportunity to work in the group. There are fewer distractions. Satan has less of an opportunity to get in and mess things up. The meeting flows smoothly, allowing Christ and His work to be the focus of the group, not the mechanics of the questions or activities.

Preparation will also build confidence. A leader who is prepared knows that the atmosphere will be ripe for an effective discussion of the Scriptures and practical application. During the meeting, the prepared leader is free to enjoy the group and see God work in and through them.

People sense the value placed on something based on the time allotted it by the leader. If you fail to take the necessary time to prepare, your members will notice and have a diminished sense of the value of the group. Moreover, if the leader does not make preparation a priority, the members will not make it a priority to attend.

The same can be said for invitations to the group. If the leader does not show that they think of the week-ly meetings *outside* the meet-ing times, then members will not think to pray for one another and invite new folks.

However, when leaders show that they are prepared, the value of the group is reinforced. Preparing for your weekly meetings is of the utmost importance.

Three Key Preparations to Make Each Week

Prepare yourself

The most important element of preparation is personal preparation. As the leader of your small group, you must strive to be right with the Lord and with others. Pray, fast, repent, worship, rest, and anything else that is necessary to be personally pre-pared to lead. Nothing is more important than this.

Prepare the atmosphere

The atmosphere can make or break the meet-ing. It is best when the group leader is not acting as the host. Whether you are the host or not, insure that the home or location where you are meeting is ready. This means the meeting place is clean, comfortable, and spacious. (Do a quick review of chapter 26 on this area of preparation.)

Prepare your agenda

The elements of a healthy small group meeting cover the five practices of a healthy small group (see chapter 7). This means time needs to be allocated for community building through the use of an ice-breaker (Welcome), connecting with God through prayer or musical praise (Worship), discussion and practical application of the Bible (Word), discussing how the group will serve and minister to others (Works), and prayer concerning who and how to evangelize the lost (Witness).

Typically, an effective agenda includes time for each practice. The wise leader spends time praying and thinking through how to best accomplish each one each week with his or her apprentice(s).

Welcome:	10-15 minutes
Worship:	10-15 minutes
Word:	30-45 minutes
Works:	10-30 minutes
Witness:	15 Minutes

(The minutes shown above are general guidelines. If your group is new, you'll spend more time on the Welcome and Worship portions of the meeting. If your group has been together for three months or longer, you'll need to adjust the meeting so you invest more time in the Works and Witness portion of the meeting.)

Preparation is the foundation for your success. If you bathe yourself and the agenda in prayer each week and plan with your apprentice(s), you will find that you are relaxed and your members will see value in your small group meetings.

Action Points:

1. Spend time each day this week praying about your upcoming meeting. Ask God what He wants to accomplish through your time together.

2. Integrate each of the five practices (Welcome, Worship, Word, Works, and Witness) into your next meeting. Delegate the icebreaker and worship to other members. Ask your apprentice to plan the agenda with you, and be sure to ask which of the remaining practices he or she will facilitate.

[This chapter adapted in part from chapter five of the book, *Eight Habits of Effective Small Group Leaders* by Dave Earley, Houston TX: Touch Publications, 2001.]

Chapter 34

Never Underestimate the Importance of a Good Party

By Dave

Everyone loves parties. From little kids getting excited about a birthday party, to teenage boys who actually bathe and use deodorant before going to a boy-girl party, to young ladies all a twitter at bridal showers, everyone loves a party! From wedding receptions and anniversaries to tailgate gatherings, getting together with good friends and tasty food is a can't-miss recipe for fun.

Never underestimate the importance of a good party or a social activity to build your group. In the small groups at my home church, we learned we could easily *double* our regular small group attendance with unchurched friends if the group members invited them to a party or two first.

Theme nights such as, "I Hate Winter," "Thanksgiving dinner," "Halloween Bonfire," and "Fifties Night" have been very successful for us. To gather a crowd, the key is to provide good food and play a few corny games. Unchurched people have a good time and listen intently to a few of our group members share their story of how they came to a personal relationship with Jesus. Often, decisions are made for Christ at such gatherings . . . all because we had a party.

God loves a good party

In the Bible, God went out of His way to tell His people that He wanted them to have parties on Earth. These parties certainly weren't drunken orgies. These were fun gatherings consisting of good food, good friends, and good times (Dt. 14:22-26). God loves parties so much that He commanded His children to take time off work and to faithfully enjoy godly parties together. He even ordained that the entire Jewish religious calendar be based on national parties or "feasts." God prescribed 10 such parties, or Feasts, for inclusion in the Jewish calendar. Never underestimate the importance of a good party.

Jesus did his first miracle at a wedding party (Jn. 2:1–10). He was anointed for His burial at a dinner party (Lk. 7:36–50). The Bible says that when a sinner repents, heaven throws a party (Lk. 15: 5–7, 9–10, 22–24). The Pharisees even criticized Jesus because they thought He was too interested in parties (Lk. 7:34). When Jesus spoke of the kingdom of heaven he called it a banquet party (Lk. 14:15–24).

Deepening relationships

Many people have a relational void or hole in their heart. One reason people come to small groups is to fill that social void in their lives. Don't fight it! Use it to build your group. Every few weeks, plan a social gathering as either part of your group's meeting schedule or on another night of the week. Such gatherings will increase the "fun quotient" of your group. Parties will add to group excitement, ownership, interest, and involvement. Parties are also very effective evangelistic tools as non-believers see firsthand that Christians can actually have fun.

Lesson #34: Social activities are a great way to grow your group.

Social gatherings provide group members with a new outlet to share even more of their lives together. During a well-planned social gathering, people often discuss things that never seem to come up in a group meeting where everyone in the room is listening to the person talk. One way to take people to a deeper relational level rapidly is through a social gathering. They get to see each other as "real people." Going rafting or playing softball allows the group members to see sides of one another that they may rarely see in the group meeting.

Discipleship opportunities

Some of Jesus' greatest moments with His disciples were not in formal settings but in social gatherings. Jesus used every opportunity to disciple His group by telling stories and asking probing questions to get His disciples to think and process what He may have said in a sermon they heard days before. You too can disciple your members the way Jesus did with conversations and dialog surrounding what you are learning as a group and as a church, based on what your pastor is sharing from the pulpit.

Retaining visitors and new members

Research shows that if new people at a church or group do not make seven friends within the first seven weeks of attendance, they will not stay. Small groups and social gatherings are the natural solution. Use social gatherings as an opportunity to help new people make friends with the others in your group quickly. Organize some type of social gathering at least every seven weeks and focus on getting new folks there as the main reason to hold the event.

The sky is the limit

There is practically no limit to what you can do for fun as a group. You can have a group picnic, go to a baseball game, have a married couple's date night, go camping, have a cookout, go bowling, play volleyball, go out to eat at a nice restaurant, play board games, and so much more. Just make sure you invite as many unchurched people and unconnected church members as possible.

Action Points:
1. At your next meeting, share with your group what you have learned from this chapter.

2. Then, as a group, plan a party where you can enjoy each other and invite unconnected people from your church, friends, coworkers, and neighbors.

3. Ask someone in your group if they'd be willing to share a 2-minute testimony at the party and help them rehearse it so they're prepared and confident. Challenge them to share what it means to be a Christian *today*, not just to describe the commitment they made to Christ, which may have been as a child or a long time ago.

Chapter 35

You Can't Have Babies If You Don't Get Pregnant

By Dave

Jim led a group for several years. It was a strong group that met the needs of the members and reached out to unchurched people. Yet, he never found an apprentice to mentor. One day, Jim had a stroke and was physically unable to lead his group any longer. Since there was no one mentored to take his place, his group closed. Looking back, Jim did nearly everything right, except mentor an apprentice.

Rod led a group for several years. It was a strong group that met the needs of the members. Unlike Jim, Rod mentored an apprentice named Scott. When Rod moved on to plant a new group, Scott took over. The group continued to grow. Over the years, Scott mentored apprentices like Mike, Mark, Dave, Dale, and Jamal. Eventually, they all led their own groups. Many of their apprentices became leaders. Mike and Jamal went on to plant new churches.

For Jim, his small group was his main priority. Rod and Scott made mentoring a priority as well as loving the members of their group and they multiplied their group several times.

Just cooperate with God

It is a huge relief when we understand that it's not entirely up to us to develop leaders. God is already in the leader-making business. Our responsibility is to simply cooperate with Him in the work He is already doing in someone's life.

Mentoring is the way one ordinary person can reach thousands

You might say, "I could never minister to a thousand people!" But if you are an effective small group leader, you can mentor someone else to become a leader. By mentoring one highly effective leader at a time, you can eventually minister to thousands through the ministry of the leaders you have trained.

Mentoring is letting go of ministry in order to let others minister

People fail to see their ministries grow because they hang on to them tightly. The problem with doing ministry by yourself is that no others are developed and the ministry stops with you. Effective mentoring involves giving away your current ministry in order to let others minister while you teach them and watch them learn and gain confidence. In other words, mentoring lets others get in on the fun of seeing God use them to change people's lives. Effective small group leaders learn to enjoy the ministry success of others as much or more than their own ministry success.

Mentoring is all about keeping leader and group multiplication a priority

One of Satan's favorite ways to keep leaders from mentoring is to get them so caught up with the "tyranny of the urgent" that they miss the long-term important things that matter most. Don't get so caught up in the moment of being a small group leader that you fail to mentor others to do

Lesson #35: Effective leaders consistently mentor others to lead new groups.

what you do. Effective mentors make the choice to mentor and keep it a priority even when small group leadership becomes hectic.

Mentoring is the most lasting part of the ministry of small group leadership

I have led small groups for thirty years. The thing I look back on is not the specific groups I have led, but the leaders I have developed … especially those who are effectively mentoring others. I count church leaders, pastors, and full-time missionaries amongst those I have had the privilege of mentoring. Their ministry has continued long after I have moved on to new areas of ministry and I have left a rich legacy of leaders in my path.

Mentoring suggestions:
- Never do ministry alone. Bring a small group member with you whenever possible.
- Take advantage of all the training opportunities

your church offers, bringing a potential leader with you to each event.

- Constantly look for new leaders. They're all around you and you'll see them if you are praying each day in this regard.
- Talk of leadership as a privilege, not a burden. Let God carry the big problems you may face as you lead your small group.
- Don't put yourself on a pedestal or good people will shy away from leadership.
- Give a potential leader responsibilities *before* you ask the person to consider leadership in your group.
- Always consult with those above you before you give a member the title of "apprentice" or "intern." Your coach or pastor may ask you to wait or choose a different person for the role.
- Realize that failing to mentor will always mean failing to multiply your personal ministry as a small group leader and the group itself.
- Do not release leaders until they have a good chance of succeeding.
- As you move through the first six months of small group life, purposely allow your ministry role to decrease and your apprentice's role to increase. This will give him or her confidence and prevent you from experiencing burnout.
- Give lavish affirmation and encouragement to your apprentices each step along the way, even when they fail. This battles discouragement.

Action Points:

1. If you have an apprentice, call them right now and tell them how much you appreciate them and what a great leader they are becoming. They can never hear enough praise from you!

2. If you don't have an apprentice, consider fasting one meal each day this week to pray and seek God's face for whom you should develop into a future leader. (Yes, it's important enough of an issue to miss a few meals to hear clearly from God!)

[This chapter is adapted from chapter six of the book, *Eight Habits of Effective Small Group Leaders* by Dave Earley, (Houston TX: Touch Publications, 2001)]

Chapter 36

Personal Growth: The Fountainhead of Long Term Effectiveness

By Dave

Wes was a great small group leader. A whirling dervish of activity, he consistently invited new people to his group and contacted his members. He was also used by God to raise up several apprentices who became effective group leaders. He loved to minister and pour himself out in service.

However, after a few years, he began to feel empty. His group was becoming stale. At the same time, he was experiencing problems with his health and his weight. Things were not always happy at home, and his children were wandering spiritually and making poor choices. He felt tired all the time, and his sunny personality disappeared. He was losing his passion for God, wondering what on earth could be wrong.

His small group coach challenged him to set up a personal growth plan. It included activities to keep his "spiritual tank" full. It addressed his diet and exercise needs. The plan also included regular time spent investing in his marriage and children. Wes began to grow again. Within a few months, he felt much better. Things began to pick up at home and in his group. His ministry was rekindled, and his effectiveness reached an entirely new level.

Through this spiritual drought, Wes learned one of the most powerful lessons any effective leader — especially a small group leader — can learn: Personal growth is the fountainhead of long-term effectiveness.

> *Nothing is more effective when it comes to reaching potential than commitment to personal growth.*
> — John Maxwell

Most things are out of our control. About the only thing you can directly improve is yourself. When you do improve yourself, everything else within your sphere of influence begins to get better. When you grow yourself as the leader, you allow God to grow your group and your people through you. You could say that the key to changing the group is changing the leader; the key to improving the group is improving the leader; and the key to growing the group is growing the leader.

Paul told Timothy, *"Train yourself to be godly"* (1 Timothy 4:7). No one else could do it for him. As Christians, we understand that we are not the victims of our environment. We have learned that what we are is more the product of our decisions than our conditions. God says that we will have to give an account of ourselves when we stand before Him (Romans 14:12). No one else is responsible for our personal growth. No one else can grow for us, learn for us, or improve for us. We have to grow, learn, and develop for ourselves.

Highly effective leaders know the value of investing in their own personal growth. They intentionally plan to maintain and grow their spiritual lives. They build time into their schedules to help them grow as a leader and as a person.

> **Lesson #36: Personal growth is not optional for the successful small group leader.**

The story has been told of a young man was hired to cut down trees as a lumberjack. The more trees he cut down, the more he was paid. Although he had never done it before, he was confident because he was big, strong, in great shape, and willing to work hard.

The first day, he got right to work and cut down ten trees. The next day, he went right to work and cut down eight. The third day, he was only able to fell six trees. The fourth day, his total was four. The fifth day, he only cut down three. He was discouraged. He had worked just as long and hard each day, yet his daily total kept declining.

He noticed that during the same week, an older, skinnier, yet more experienced lumberjack cut down nine trees each day. The new lumberjack approached the experienced man and said, "Let me ask you two questions: First, why were you able to do the same amount each day and my total kept declining? Second, I got right to work each morning and you didn't. What were you doing?"

The lumberjack smiled and said, "I can answer both questions with one answer. Each morning, I take time to sharpen my axe."

Are you sharpening your ax each morning?

Highly effective leaders know the value of "sharpening their axe." They take time each morning to meet with God in prayer and time in the Word. They build time for exercise and reading into their schedules. They don't neglect their families. They watch less TV than others because they are joyfully finding fulfillment in their personal growth and development. Are you investing in yourself enough to sustain ministry to others?

Action Points:

1. Write down everything you do each day in broad categories for the next few weeks. At the end of each day, take ten minutes to take inventory of the following:

   - How many hours you worked and slept.

   - How many minutes of TV you watched.

   - How many minutes you spent with your spouse and each child.

   - How much time you spent reading for pleasure or knowledge.

   - What you ate at each meal.

   - How much you exercised.

   - How much time you prayed and spent time in the Word.

   - How much time you spent with other members of your group in person or on the phone.

2. After a few weeks, total up the categories and determine what's lacking and make changes. Then share your plan of action with your coach or pastor so they can pray for you and hold you accountable.

Chapter 37

The First Command Has Yet to be Fulfilled

By Dave

Genesis is the book of beginnings. Every major truth recorded in the Bible appears in embryonic form in Genesis. This includes the first command ever given to mankind.

> So God created man in His own image; in the image of God He created him; male and female He created them. Then God blessed them, and God said to them, *"Be fruitful and multiply…"*
>
> (Gen. 1:27–28, NASB)

This command given to Adam and Eve was focused primarily on *biological* multiplication. Mankind has done a fairly good job of filling the planet with human beings. However, Jesus expanded and deepened the command by applying it to *spiritual* multiplication. He wanted His disciples to reach the world through multiplying their lives by raising up disciples who would then raise up more disciples. This command, or commission, is still waiting to be fulfilled. While it has been shared twice before in this book, it bears repeating because it's so important for all of us to embrace:

> Therefore, go and make disciples of all nations, baptizing them in the name of the Father and of the Son and of the Holy Spirit, and teaching them to obey everything I have commanded you...
>
> (Matthew 28:19-20)

The Apostle Paul made the general command very specific, and therefore dynamic, when he wrote, *"And the things that you have heard from me among many witnesses, commit these to faithful men who will be able to teach others also"* (2 Tim. 2:2 NKJV). Note that this single verse describes four "generations" of multiplication. It started with Paul (the first generation) who was addressing Timothy (second generation) who was to commit what he learned from Paul to "faithful men" (the third generation) who would teach "others" (fourth generation).

Lesson #37: We can reach our world for Christ if we consistently develop leaders.

The commands to multiply, to make disciples, and to commit what we have learned to others should ring in our ears and resonate in our hearts until we obey. God desires that everyone on the planet comes into a soul-saving, life-changing relationship with Him. They will only be reached as we multiply our lives into others.

On any given Sunday, I am preaching in New

York City, Chicago, Trucksville (a town in Pennsylvania), and Columbus. This is true in that I have tried to multiply my life into pastors who have started churches in those places. I also tell people, tongue in cheek, that by raising up small group leaders, I can lead small groups all over Columbus without leaving my home. Case in point, Rod and I started a small group in 1985. By 2002, there were 125 small groups because we multiplied leaders who also multiplied themselves into others.

The Power of Multiplication

Below is a chart that shows something of the power of multiplication to make an impact. It depicts how many small group leaders, including you, will exist based on various levels of multiplication. While

	No Training	If you train ONE multiplier each year	If you train TWO multipliers each year
1 Year	1 (You)	1 new leader + Yourself = 2 leaders	2 new leaders + Yourself = 3
2 Years	1 (You)	2 leaders + 2 leaders (each one trains one) = 4 leaders	3 leaders + 6 leaders (each one trains two) = 9 leaders
3 Years	1 (You)	4 leaders + 4 leaders = 8	9 leaders + 18 leaders = 27 leaders
4 Years	1 (You)	8 leaders + 8 leaders = 16	27 leaders + 54 leaders = 81 leaders
10 Years	1 (You)	1520 Leaders!	59,049 Leaders!

it is idealistic, it illustrates an important point.

If it appears too far-fetched, realize that the strongest churches in the world have *tens of thousands of members* in *thousands* of small groups. Never underestimate the power of multiplication. You can do it, or better yet, God can do it through you. Three questions remain: If not you, who? If not here, where? If not now, when?

Action Point:

This week, take time to pray specifically for a vision to multiply yourself through many generations of ordinary people who will selflessly serve an extraordinary God.

Chapter 38

Stages of Maturity
for Small Groups
By Rod

Have you ever taken the time to look and marvel at the beauty of a butterfly? Every now and then one will fly by and I will say to myself, "That is beautiful!" In order for that butterfly to become amazing, it must go through four different stages of maturity called *metamorphosis*. The first stage is the egg. The second stage is called the caterpillar, larva, or the nutritive stage. The third stage is called the pupal stage, and is a time of great transition. This is a time when the caterpillar rests and changes dramatically inside a cocoon. The final stage is the adult or reproductive stage. This stage is where the ugly, slow, cumbersome caterpillar develops wings and flies away as a beautiful butterfly, pollinating flowers and reproducing itself.

If you have been a group leader for any length of time, you'll see some of the similarities between the development of a butterfly and the metamorphosis of an ordinary small group. Hopefully, the group will develop to the point where it reproduces itself many times over. This transition—whenever it occurs—is equally awe-inspiring.

Every group goes through stages. The stages are either healthy or they are unhealthy. In any case, it is helpful to recognize and respond to the common signs found in each stage.

The formation stage

This is the initial stage for the group and lasts approximately two months. During this period, group members are getting to know one another and the members do not yet consider this group to be "my group." During this stage, it's important that the leader sets the tone and clearly explains the goals and mission of the group so the members can band together and achieve the goals.

The exploration stage

This stage is where the members begin to see what group life is about. At this phase of group life, it's common for members to question the leader (and the leadership team) regarding the group's purpose. This stage typically lasts two to four months. During this time, the wise leader will reiterate the mission of the group to show his or her desire to lead the group into achieving something big for God.

The execution stage

During the third stage, the group is healthy and is interested in becoming and doing what the leader and the leadership team has been casting a vision to do. This is the "achievement stage" which occurs during months five through nine. When a group moves into this stage, the members are busy serving one another, inviting unchurched friendsto the group or parties, and living in biblical community.

The preparation stage

The fourth stage, like the metamorphosis of the caterpillar, is a stage of rest. However, inside the group … deep changes are taking place. The group is now naturally growing and adding new people on a regular basis without a lot of extra work. The members are maturing spiritually and new leaders are being released to serve and care for the members and facilitate various parts of the meetings. This stage occurs during months 9-12.

> Lesson #38: Just like a caterpillar becomes a butterfly, your group will go through big changes.

The multiplication stage

This stage can also be called "birthing stage." As the name implies, this is a time when the group becomes two or more groups. Often, some pain accompanies this stage. However, the ultimate joy of reproducing a new group outweighs the struggles of birth. This stage typically occurs during months 12 through 18 in a healthy group. The primary leader invites a handful of members to start a new group, or one of the new leaders leaves the cocoon with others and a new group is formed.

The stages above describe a small group where

the members rally around the goals of the group and the leader is strong, yet loving and sensitive. The leader of this group, like the butterfly, understands how important reproduction is for the survival of the species and works hard to raise up other leaders from within the group.

The distortion stage

Unfortunately, there is one more stage of small group life that will happen to groups that do not grow and develop leaders within 18-24 months. After this much time together, a group loses its momentum and the vision to multiply. If the group has been together for two years, it is in danger of dying and needs immediate attention to refocus the efforts toward growth and multiplication.

The action points in this chapter (found on the following page) are especially important. Take time right now to ponder each question and work with your coach and group to move to the next level. As you answer the questions, remember that healthy groups that multiply are as beautiful as any butterfly that you will ever see!

Action Points:

1. What stage is your group in right now? How long has it been in that stage? Write your answers below:

2. What do you think your group needs to move to the next stage?

3. In what ways are you developing your members to lead a group of their own one day?

4. When do you see your current group multiplying?

Chapter 39

How to Help a Potential Leader Move Around The Bases

By Rod

Everyone knows that baseball is America's favorite pastime. Part of the reason for its popularity is the simplicity of the game. The basic concept of trying to get a player to make it to home base and score a run is fun and exciting. Don't you remember the joy and pure pleasure of crossing home the first time you played? Every time a player crosses home plate there is a celebration because it means that your team is making progress and may even win the game if enough runs are scored.

There are many joys in small group ministry; making new friends, teaching the Word, praying for one another and sharing life together. One of the greatest joys, however, is when you see someone who has been a part of your group grow and develop to the point where he or she begins a new group. If you think scoring a run in baseball is cool, wait until you experience the thrill of one of "yours" crossing home plate and starting his or her group!

The way baseball teams develop new players is through an extensive training regimen and a farm club system. The way small groups develop new leaders is much the same way. First you need some kind of a training plan that is a combination of instruction and mentoring. The instruction can come, if your church has it, in the form of "core" classes. Rick Warren and the *Purpose-Driven Church* made this base path development popular.

Lesson #39:
The greatest joy in small group ministry is developing and releasing someone else to lead a new group.

Again, the basic concept is simple. First, identify four points or goals that you want every leader to accomplish with the fourth objective being the leader starting a new group. The first three goals culminate in that one purpose.

First base could be selecting an apprentice for your group. Remember to look for someone who has F.A.I.T.H. This acrostic stands for someone who is faithful, able, has integrity, is teachable, and has a heart for God. (See chapter 24 for more information regarding this person.)

Second base could be establishing a regular meeting time with your apprentice. It could be a breakfast meeting on the day of the meeting or you could meet an hour before the group meets for prayer and planning.

Third base could be setting S.M.A.R.T. goals for your group. This acrostic stands for specific, measurable, awe-inspiring, relevant, and timed goals. Growth goals, service goals, and multiplication goals are a few areas to consider.

Home plate is starting a new group with your blessing and prayers. You may want to have a party where you pray for and bless the new group leader and the new core group. This is a time of celebration and vision casting for all the other potential leaders in the two groups!

Baseball is simple to understand and it is popular with the American public because we can measure where we are in the contest. It is divided into innings. There are just four bases. Runs are scored when a player crosses home plate. The team with the most runs wins. The basic idea of small group leadership development is much the same as winning baseball philosophy ... "get 'em on ... get 'em around ... and get 'em home!"

Action Points:

1. Which of the four bases do you need to work on with potential leaders?

2. Try to identify where the members of your group are in relation to the four bases. What step do they need to take next?

Chapter 40

What Should You Report to Your Pastor or Coach?

By Rod

Hebrews 13:17 says, *"Obey your leaders, and submit to them; for they keep watch over your souls, as those who will give an account. Let them do this with joy and not with grief, for this would be unprofitable for you"* (NASB). This verse implies that leaders will give an account of those persons they serve. As a small group leader, try to put yourself in the shoes of your pastor or coach who has oversight of your group. What are some things you would like to know about your small groups? Here are ten questions to answer when discussing your small group with your pastor or coach:

1. *What are some good things that have happened in your group?* Everyone likes to hear a good report. Your coach or pastor is no exception. Take a look at some of the recent answered prayers and praise God for them by sharing this information. Or, listen carefully to how people are growing spiritually and make a note of it to pass along. This will also help you to remain positive in mind and heart as a leader.

2. *What are the challenges faced by those in your care?* Without using names of violating confidences... share the common concerns from the members in your small group. This will help your leadership know how to minister to the whole congregation with counseling needs, sermon series, and the ability to intercede on behalf of your group members.

3. *How is your apprentice development coming along?* Who are you training and what are you doing? Also cover what core classes your apprentice has taken or milestones they have achieved. These points are good indications that you are developing someone to birth a new group in the near future, which is always beautiful music to the ears of a pastor or coach.

4. *How is the host location working out?* Your coach or pastor needs to know whether or not things are working out in your present meeting location. If there's a problem, he or she can help you find a better place and/or time to meet.

5. *How healthy are your key relationships?* If you have an unhealthy or imbalanced relationship with your spouse, child, or a member of your group, it will have a negative impact on your ministry. Your coach or pastor needs to know if a significant conflict has arisen in your relationships. Remember, he or she is on your side and wants the best for you.

6. *Who is your group praying for to receive salvation?* This question is meant to remind and impress you—the small group leader—to keep your group focused on the fact that "lost people are important to God." Share the first names of the people you are trying to relate to and speak frankly about the amount of prayer your group is doing today.

7. *Are you achieving your group's growth goals?* What goals have you set for the group, and how are you progressing toward the accomplishment of those goals? This is a question that your coach or pastor would like to know so they can help you succeed. Share praises and challenges you face in this area and watch them rally behind you.

> Lesson #40: Sharing as much as you can with your pastor or coach will help them know how to support you.

8. *Has your group incorporated new people this month?* Again, the focus here is on reaching new people for your group. This question is designed to help you keep a clear outreach goal in mind. Discussing this with your coach or pastor may also jog their memory as to new people they have met in church services that would be a great fit for your group.

9. *How is your group's participation level?* Group participation—in meetings and between meetings—is a key component to a healthy group. If members are not participating, it is very important to discuss this and ask your pastor or coach to help you get your group interacting with one another.

10. *How is the group's prayer level?* A praying group is God-dependent. Honestly assess this and let your coach or pastor know how the commitment to prayer is developing in your group.

When you lead a small group, you are actually representing the leaders in your church. Therefore, it is vital that you keep them up-to-date and informed as to what is happening in your group. It is also important to let your leaders know what kind of leadership you are providing to those allotted to your charge. Meet with your pastor or coach as often as you can to bring them up to speed on the praises and challenges you see in your group. You will feel supported and they will gain the knowledge they need to respond in powerful ways.

Action Points:

1. Ask your coach or pastor if you can meet them for coffee one evening or breakfast once a month to discuss these questions. Plan a regular time and place to do this, even if it has to be moved from time to time to make it work.

2. Before you next meet with your pastor or coach, re-read this chapter and write out the answers to the ten questions. This will help you remain focused and keep your time together powerful and brief.

Chapter 41

Ministering to Difficult People In Your Meetings

By Rod

We've all had "one of those kind of people" in our groups. This person has the special ability to "hijack" your small group. Every time you meet, it seems as if he or she has taken everyone in the group "hostage" with his or her particular viewpoint, need, hurt, or strong personality. It's enough to drive a small group and the leader crazy!

Years ago I had a difficult person like this in the first group I led. JoAnne came into the group through the invitation of a friend. The first night, I could tell we had a problem on our hands. There was no question, prayer request, or passage where she could not resist sharing her vast knowledge. I figured that it was her first week in our group and she may have just wanted to let everyone know her story. After a couple of weeks, it didn't get better. She over-spoke with great authority at every opportunity and I knew I had to do something. I consulted some of the books I had on small groups and each one advised me to talk to JoAnne before or after the group, reviewing the nature and purpose of the group. I needed to communicate that one of the goals of group life is to try and get everyone involved. If the group has one person dominating the discussion and time, then others don't get to participate.

The next week, JoAnne and I visited about these very things and this seemed to work for a while. A few weeks later, she had a relapse and it was back to group domination. Wondering what to do next, I did more research. Here is what I found to help a dominating group member like JoAnne.

Redirect the discussion

When one or two group members are monopolizing the discussion, calling for contributions from others often helps. Use questions like, "What do the rest of you think?" or "Jack, what ideas do you have about this?"

> **Lesson #41: There will always be a difficult person in your group. Prayer and a desire to help are your keys to helping them grow.**

You may be able to enlist the monopolizing member to help you draw in others. Ask the person to redirect questions they hear during the evening to the quiet people or those who have yet to contribute to the group discussion. This may help him or her become more sensitive to the contributions of others. In some situations, you may have to take control of the discussion in a strong way and speak privately with the dominant member after the meeting, explaining the necessity of group participation.

Recognition of wandering

A verbal recognition of the fact that the member is "chasing rabbits" can usually help you get back to more relevant topics. You could say, "This is interesting. However, we've left our topic. Perhaps we could discuss this further after the group. For now, let's focus on...." Or, you may present a thought-provoking question to draw the discussion back to the initial topic. Maintaining an attitude of acceptance toward the tangent is important. This shows respect for each member's opinion.

Responding to "wrong" answers

If someone says something that you are quite sure is inaccurate or unbiblical, you may want to solicit a second viewpoint from someone else: "What do the rest of you think?" or "Does anyone know other Scripture passages that may help us here?" You might restate the issue, or ask another question that would help clarify or stimulate further thought. Always try to keep the person from losing "face" or becoming embarrassed.

Reaffirming silence

Don't be afraid of pauses or try to fill silent moments or you may be the difficult person who dominates in your group. If you give everyone time to think, they will bring up good points and ask good questions as the discussion progresses. By being patient, you may be surprised with the number of excellent thoughts your members will voice. These silent times may seem uncomfortable, but don't be embarrassed or feel as if you must say something. A short period of silence during ministry time also gives your members time to listen to the Holy Spirit and respond in transparency. Silence is indeed golden.

Responding to difficult questions honestly

Another excellent way to avoid dominating in your group is to say, "I don't know" when a difficult question is raised. If you don't know the answer, don't pretend you do! You can always look for the answer later, or ask someone else in the group to research it. There is no merit in being thought of as a supposed "know it all", only to find out you don't. This also models excellent leadership to others in your group. If they understand that good leadership is not "all-knowing," they'll be far more comfortable with a leadership role.

Facilitating a group is inherently difficult. After all, you are dealing with people. They are complex, needy, and sometimes hurting. You need wisdom and patience to handle difficult personalities. Praying for these members each day, asking God to show you how to speak to them and minister to them will overcome discouragement. If you love people with Christ's love, it will come through and they will know you are doing your best to help them and everyone else in the group.

Action Points:

1. Do you have any challenging personalities in your group? Take time to pray for them now, asking God to give you His love for them and his insight into how to best minister to them.

2. Which of the suggestions in this article do you want to put into practice right away? Write it here in your own words to help you remember to do it.

Chapter 42

How to Integrate Children Into Your Meetings

By Rod

When I get to heaven, I hope I will be able to go back and review some of the more important dates in history. The wonders of creation, God appearing to Abraham, Samson defeating the Philistines, Daniel in the Lion's den, Jonah and the whale, and the resurrection of our Lord and Savior. Another fascinating day that I would love to re-examine is the Day of Pentecost and the days just after the start of the church age. Specifically, I want to hear and view the initial conversations of how they were going to structure this new gathering of people. The particular issue I would be curious to know is what on earth did they do with all those children while they met together?

The early church didn't have Sunday School or Junior Church. There were no publishing houses cranking out curriculum that followed a scope and sequence. There were no elaborate facilities that had indoor and outdoor play areas. What did they do?

If you are a small group leader, you probably face this same dilemma. You may not have thousands of children, but the half-dozen that you do have can certainly cause frustration for the entire group if you don't make preparations for them. Following are some ideas I have found to work in my church and other churches with whom I associate.

Integration options

Group integration has worked in a number of churches, but it takes lots of planning and patience. There are two ways to incorporating your children into meetings (as opposed to off-site childcare or babysitting).

The first option is to plan for the children to take part in the first part of the meeting, including the icebreaker, worship, and the prayer time. Children under 12 — though this varies from church to church — are then invited to go to the back yard or another part of the house for a Bible lesson and activity. The older children, youth, and adults move into the Bible study and application time. In this first option, it is important that the members of your group are willing to take their turn working with the children, and that the parents are comfortable with the adults and youth who may be in another part of the house with their children.

The second option is to keep the children of all ages in the meeting and help them learn to participate. This second option requires a great deal of patience on the part of the parents, but is highly rewarding. Seeing a six-year-old praying for an adult's healing or sharing a prayer request for another child they know from their neighborhood makes the adjustment period worthwhile.

If your church does not have a children's pastor

who can help you integrate your children into your meetings (and you should ask for help if you do have a children's pastor), here are some additional ideas to help you:

Lesson #42: Involving the children in your meetings may be the most powerful thing they ever experience.

- Ask your youth minister to help you find responsible teenagers in your church to provide childcare and pay them for their time. The costs involved should be divided between the parents based on the total number of children being cared for during the meetings.

- Are there mature adults in your church whose grandchildren live far away? Ask them to play with and care for the children during the meetings, perhaps in return for more difficult chores done around their homes by your group.

Customize your plan of action

Each small group is different and has different needs, especially in relationship to the age of the children. A single childcare or integration plan may not fit every small group. Don't hesitate to visit with your coach or pastor if you need some "outside the box" solutions for working with children in your groups.

Small groups can be a great opportunity for the children to learn and grow as well as the adults.

Since the kids see each other every week, some of their best friendships may blossom in the group among other children as well as a dozen or more adopted "aunts and uncles." Work hard to involve your children in your meetings and in relationship to other members of your group outside meeting times. They will discover their spiritual purpose in life early and lead full, productive lives building God's kingdom.

Action Points:

1. In an upcoming small group meeting, as some-one to read Mark 10:13-16. Then ask your group these questions:
   a. What stands out to you in this passage?
   b. What words characterize the disciples' attitude toward children, and what words characterize Jesus' words?
   c. How did Jesus specifically love and minister to the children?

2. Now ask someone to read Mark 9:37 and ask this follow up question: Based on Jesus' words in this passage, how well are we doing as a small group to welcome Christ? Are we rejecting, tolerating or welcoming Him (and our children) or somewhere in between? Why?

3. Next, take time to pray as a group, committing yourselves to minister to and *with* your children in a greater way.

4. As a wrap up, discuss practical things you can put into action in the next few weeks to increase the level of child participation in and out of meetings.

[The small group guide in the Action Points of this chapter were taken from *Cell Group Leader Training* by M. Scott Boren and Don Tillman, (Houston, TX, Cell Group Resources), p. 122]

Chapter 43

The Balance Between Outreach and Inreach

By Rod

Every four years during the summer Olympic Games, there is an event called the balance beam. You're probably familiar with the event. The beam is a piece of wood that is 4 inches wide and 12 feet long, perched 42 inches off the ground. The allure of watching this Olympic sport is the amazing feats of balance the athletes display while performing their routines. The best athletes have trained to the point where they look comfortable as they jump, twirl, and flip through the air on the narrow beam. The truly outstanding performers do all this and "stick the landing" as the crowd roars its approval.

In a small group environment there is a similar balancing act. The balancing act that every group should work to achieve is the exhortation from Christ to keep our eyes on the harvest fields (Matthew 9:36-38) and the goal to develop community in every group (John 13:34-35).

If you have led a group for any length of time, you know that balancing between outreach and inreach requires the skills of an Olympian. Here are some pointers to accomplish this from a teammate who has fallen off the balance beam (of mission and comfort) more than a few times.

Talk and pray about the balance frequently

As your group is forming, make sure you create a group covenant. (Review chapter 21 for details.) The covenant should include things like availability, commitment, confidentiality, and goals for outreach and multiplication. From day one, make sure group members understand that one of the purposes of the group is to reach out to friends, family members, coworkers, and neighbors as well as caring for group members.

Lesson #43: Healthy small groups focus on both outreach and community.

Strategically invest time during your meetings to pray for local people who have yet to trust Christ. Additionally, make sure there is at least one empty chair in your circle so your group can see that you have room for new group members. One final suggestion is to periodically talk about multiplication. Remind your group members that the natural progression of life, no matter how painful, is to birth new life.

Once a group is established, the strategic-minded leader will attempt to accomplish the "one another" commands which result in biblical community. Developing community, however, can quickly degenerate to being overly comfortable. Comfort is a by-product of taking one's eyes off the harvest fields. It happens easily enough. All one has to do is stop looking outward and sure enough, he or she will gravitate toward a stagnant often state called "us four and no more."

Maintaining the balance requires practice

Much like the Olympic athlete, the accomplished leader will develop to the point where reaching new people, incorporating them into the group, and developing leaders is made to look easy. Disciplined leaders "stick the landing" and multiply the group, while balancing, back and forth, between mission and comfort. Your twofold goal is to bring your members together so they can reach out and grow.

Action Points:

1. In what ways are you helping your members develop biblical community and become friends between meetings? Jot down your thoughts here.

2. What can you do in the next few weeks to cast a vision for reaching out to bring balance to your group? (Use the next page to write out your ideas.) If ideas don't come to mind, consider asking your group to brainstorm with you.

Chapter 44

How Will You Know If Your Group is Growing?

By Rod

Certain types of growth are a difficult thing to gauge. There is no single indicator that you can look at and say, "That's it!" or, "This is the key." However, with small group growth, there are two simple indicators that measure growth: the spiritual growth of each member and the numerical growth of your group. If both of these things are happening, your group is probably healthy.

Spiritual growth

Spiritual growth is measured by walking in the Spirit and growing in maturity. Indicators like love, joy, peace, patience, gentleness, goodness, and faithfulness reveal to others that the nature of Christ is being transferred from the Spirit into our daily living. Other indicators of spiritual growth are evidenced by our willingness to serve others and to help them come to know Christ in a personal way. Yet another indicator of growth in spiritual maturity is discovering and using the spiritual gifts that God has entrusted to us.

What about the people in your group? How is their spiritual growth coming along? You must devote yourself to the Word and to prayer, then help others in your group do the same to see spiritual growth. Take time to get to know each member, and share what you are learning from the Word and through prayer. Ask them what they are learning, and encourage them to seek God's purpose for their life through reading their Bible, studying, learning more about their faith, and devoting themselves to prayer.

Numerical growth

Numerical growth is much easier to measure, but it is equally challenging to accomplish. Leading a small group is like juggling. The more things you get moving, the more success you will see. Let's take a look at several suggestions to grow your group numerically, keeping in mind that numbers are not everything, but they are important.

1. Pray for new people during your devotional time each day. Let me remind you that nothing of eternal significance ever happens apart from prayer. You should be setting the example for the people entrusted to your care by praying for others.

2. Ask your members whom they could invite to your group. Make a list of the names and begin praying for those people to join you. When you visit with your members between meetings, ask about the people on the list and how you can pray for them specifically.

3. If you have a prayer team in your church, turn in the names of the people you are praying for and ask the prayer team to pray for these future members.

4. Invest some time to pray in each meeting. It is very important to not only talk about prayer, but it is important to *actually pray* for new people.

Lesson #44: Small group growth can be measured with spiritual and numeric milestones.

5. Use Sunday morning to "go fishing" for new members. If your church is a gathering place for new people, train your members to look around and initiate conversations with people who are new to the church. You should not overwhelm people that visit your church, but you should be affable. The Bible tells us that if we want to have friends, "a man must show himself friendly."

6. Pay attention to new members who have recently joined your church. If your church has a membership class, why not join the class or show up early with a member from your group, inviting them to your small group?

7. Invite new people from the community to your group regularly. Remember this statement from Dave in an earlier chapter, "If you invite them,

they will come." Here's another one, "No guests, no growth." Motto's like this help remind us of our priorities, so feel free to share them with your group.

8. Set monthly or quarterly growth goals and work to accomplish them. Again, this is a matter of prayer and your group's core members need to agree on this, but it important to set some simple, yet attainable goals. After all, goals have the power to keep us moving in the right direction.

9. Cast the vision to start a new group from your group within one year.

Small group leadership is great fun and rewarding when you see spiritual growth in your members *and* your group grows in numbers. Focus on these two things in balance and you're on your way!

Action Points:

1. Buy a journal and write down the names of each of your members on a page of their own. Then write down how you are praying for their spiritual walk. Use this to record praise reports, breakthroughs, and requests. This will naturally help you encourage your members to grow spiritually when you are together.

2. Call your pastor or the church office and ask for a list of new members who have yet to visit a

small group. Call them on Saturday afternoon and invite them to lunch after church. If you can bring along one or two other members of your group, you'll find friendships will form quickly and they'll visit your group right away. When you've gained some self confidence in inviting new members, move to visitors to your services and then unchurched friends and family with on-the-spot invitations.

Chapter 45

Leader Burnout:
Healing and Prevention

By Rod

You know you should prepare your teaching or call one of your small group members, but you just don't do it. You know you should go the leader's meeting, but you just don't want to go. You know you should spend some extra time in prayer for your group, but watching T.V. is a higher priority. The fire is gone. Your "get up and go" got up and went! You have lost your motivation to lead your small group.

When you recognize these symptoms in yourself, it is important to take tangible and immediate steps to reverse the situation. One of Satan's favorite tools is discouragement. When you face discouragement as a leader, you must learn to deal with it sooner rather than later. Let's face it; we all become discouraged at times. What you do with that discouragement will determine your usability in the kingdom of God. If not addressed early, discouragement can quickly spiral into depression. To recognize and respond accordingly, here are three suggestions from the Spirit to the church of Ephesus, found in Revelation 2:1-7.

"Remember… from where you have fallen."

Go back in your mind and recall the early days of leading your group and the excitement of watching God use you to encourage believers "to grow in their most holy faith." Recall the joy of listening to people in your group pray aloud for the first time. Recollect the passion of your early prayer meetings for the lost and hurting. Remember the first time someone in your group followed the Lord in baptism. Review in your mind someone who has left your group to work in another city, and is serving the Lord in another church.

"Repent of leaving your first love" (the God of the Word and the Word of God).

Set aside extra time for the life-changing and Spirit-quickening Word of God. Like taking a drink of cold water on a hot day, your spirit will be restored as you spend time by the streams of living water. You didn't mean to get away from the Word, but you did. Come back to a daily intake of its life-giving water!

"Repeat the deeds you did at first."

In addition to spending time in the Word, *"Go into your inner room and pray to your Father who sees in secret. And your Father who sees in secret, will reward you in the open"* (Mt. 6:6). Also repeat the first habits of leading your small group. Inviting new people to the group, calling and contacting your members, spending time together, and just having fun are habits that are worth repeating. If you practice these things, your feelings will soon follow your good actions.

Burnout prevention

You may be asking, how can I prevent burnout from occurring in the first place? This is a little more difficult to address because it involves making sure that your spiritual gift (or gifts) are finding expression in

Lesson #45: Leader burnout occurs when we've distanced ourselves from God and we're serving outside of our gifting.

your small group leadership. If you have the gift of teaching, make sure you are exercising that teaching gift with opportunities in your church. If you have the gift of administration, then make sure you are finding an expression of that gift in or out of your group. The same is true with mercy or gifts of faith. Make sure you are operating in the realm of the Spirit's quickening dimension.

If you are ministering in the Spirit instead of your own power, then you know the truth of Phillipians 4:13 which states, *"I can do all things through Him who strengthens me."* The idea is that Christ is working in and through you when you are ministering according to the gift(s) that He has given you. Discover and embrace them as soon as possible and you'll never be burned out as a small group leader.

These suggestions taken together will not only cure burnout when it occurs, but they will prevent burnout from happening in the first place.

Action Points:

1. Are you feeling burned out or in danger of becoming burned out because you are not ministering according to your giftedness? Tell your coach or pastor you need help! Don't let a lack of motivation turn into discouragement and then become depressed. Your church leadership is in place to support you and help you find balance in ministry.

2. Do you see burnout in any of your members? Read this chapter aloud to your group when you next meet and discuss it openly. Then take time to pray for God's refreshment and wisdom as to how to work out of your spiritual giftedness.

Chapter 46

Evaluating Your Group's Success

By Rod

Whenever I ask anyone in ministry about how to evaluate ministry success the conversation invariably turns toward numbers. How many, how much, and how often are questions that are asked in the quest for bigger numbers. As a small group pastor, I have often been accused of being only interested in numbers. The reason for this is because I am passionate about people coming to know Christ, developing in Christ, and reaching their full potential for Christ. I do not and will not apologize for being interested in people. People are the ministry. This interest in people, though, makes some nervous because it can be misinterpreted as a superficial commitment to *attendance*.

The tension comes when one examines quantity and tries to measure that against *quality*. Would you rather have quantity or quality in your group? The answer is always both! In order to have quality, you must have some quantity. In order to have some quantity, you must have some quality. Group success in a large part is based upon your ability to balance these two seemingly opposite positions.

For most groups the process goes something

like this. Your group starts out small and everyone is friendly. The Bible study and application time is good because everyone is participating. Since the quality is good, the people in your group invite their friends and the group grows. Quantity increases. When your group grows beyond 12-15 people, the quality goes down because the participation level decreases in direct proportion to the increased attendance. So, as a leader you are faced with your first dilemma. How do you keep your group growing in quality and quantity?

**Lesson #46:
To succeed in small group leadership, you must focus on the quality of your group and the quantity of leaders you are producing.**

This is where the vision to multiply your group and develop new leaders comes into focus. The ultimate success for a small group leader is to simultaneously grow your group in quality, and quantity *while* developing future leaders. This is no small task. It requires a combination of spirituality, friendliness, and leadership.

In this little book, there are 51 additional chapters devoted to helping you develop all of the necessary skills and habits to effectively grow your group in quality, quantity and multiplication. Look over the previous chapter titles and identify the top three or four that you need to work on.

Working on everything will get you nowhere fast. You must focus on a few things and do them well. Then move on to other things you want to do to help your group become successful.

Action Points:

1. Which three chapters in this book are "success" chapters for you? Write them here.

2. Review the points at the end of each of the three chapters and decide how you will go about putting them into action to increase quality and quantity in your small group.

3. Share your action plan with other leaders in your church and ask them to pray for you!

Chapter 47

Catch the Vision of Multiplying Leaders

By Dave

If you met Scott, you would not be aware of the impact he has had, is having and will have on the kingdom of God. The first time we met, he introduced himself to me as "just a pizza shop guy." We spent time together, and after seeing his potential I encouraged him to become a small group leader. He agreed, went through our training process, and became a hard working leader with a growing small group.

Then Scott caught the dream of multiplication. Within a few months, he trained Mark to lead a group and helped him start a group of his own. Then he trained Dale to lead and, just like Mark, helped him start another group. Next, he trained Steve and … you get the picture. In ten years, Scott trained four small group leaders out of his group! In addition, another young man he mentored went on to plant a new church.

Scott has made quite a kingdom impact for "just a pizza shop guy." It all began when he caught the vision of making a difference by multiplying leaders.

A big vision makes a big difference

In 1987, Cesar Fajardo had a small ministry with just thirty young people in his youth group. However, Fajardo had a big dream. He took a photograph of the nearby indoor soccer stadium and hung the picture on the wall of his room. He began to dream and believe that God would one day fill it with young people. By the year 1999, there were 18,000 young people lined up on Saturday nights to get inside that stadium for his youth worship service.

Within twelve years, Cesar raised up a family of 8,000 youth small group leaders for his church in Bogotá, Colombia. His success began with a dream. His dream spurred him to pour his life into developing 12 multiplying group leaders, who in turn have each raised up twelve multiplying group leaders, and so on. He states, "The vision must take hold of your life, and you must be able to transmit that vision."[1]

Fajardo's success has eight simple, discernible elements:

- He saw it. His vision was so vivid he could take a picture of it.
- He saw it big. He saw an 18,000-seat auditorium filled with students seeking God.
- He saw it through the eyes of faith. He only had 30 kids in 1987, yet by faith he believed God would one day multiply 30 into a stadium full of young people.
- He saw himself in the picture. He believed God could use him to make it happen.

- He started where he was. He trained the 12 he had in order to get the 18,000 he did not yet have.
- He diligently poured his life into raising up others to lead. The focus of his time, energy, and effort for the next dozen years was training his twelve to multiply more "multipliers."
- He kept focused on the vision over a long period of time. He stayed with it for twelve years until the dream became a reality.
- God brought great results. The stadium was full on Saturday nights.

You can do it!

You probably aren't ready to envision 8,000 small group leaders today. But if you are an effective small group leader, there is no reason you should not be envisioning cooperating with God in raising at least one healthy, growing, effective multiplying spiritual leader a year. You can do it if you catch a dream from the Lord. Many small group leaders already possess a vision of multiplying their servant heart into others, and this is just one step further.

> Lesson #47: A vision to multiply your leadership abilities will give you passion and purpose as a small group leader.

But it is not enough to have a vision. The vision only becomes a reality when you follow through on your part and begin to pour your life into potential leaders.

Ten steps to fulfilling your vision

1. First, get with God and get His vision for your life and ministry.
2. Write it down and picture it.
3. Refer to it frequently.
4. Believe that God can and will do it.
5. Ask God to do it His way and in His timing.
6. Plan to fulfill your part.
7. Learn everything you possibly can in order to accomplish your part of the vision.
8. Work like it all depends on you. Pray like it all depends on God.
9. Start small, but speak and live like the vision is becoming a reality.
10. Don't quit.

A vision to multiply your leadership abilities will give you passion and purpose as a small group leader. It will also help you to keep growing and learning as you raise up others to minister to your small group members. And last, a vision to multiply leadership will leave a long legacy of leaders well after you have died and gone home to be with our Lord! Ask the Lord for His vision for your life as a multiplying leader and he will begin to birth that vision within you.

Action Points:

1. What is your vision for your ministry as a small group leader? Write it below. (If you don't have a clear vision for your ministry, write out a prayer asking God for a new and powerful vision for your future to develop others as leaders.)

2. Who can you tell about your vision? Your spouse? Your pastor or coach? Your group? Talking about it will help you refine and reinforce it.

Notes:
1. Joel Comiskey, *Groups of 12*, (Houston, TX: TOUCH Publications, 1999), p. 37.

[Parts of this chapter, adapted from chapter one of Dave Earley's, *Turning Members into Leaders*, (Houston, TX: TOUCH Publications, 2003).]

Chapter 48

The Key to Discovering Potential Leaders

By Dave

"How do I find someone to disciple?"

"Where will I find a potential apprentice?"

"Where will I find the people into which I am to multiply my life?"

Small group leaders often start asking these questions once they catch the vision of multiplying themselves by multiplying group leaders.

Jesus is our example in all things, including selecting potential leaders. Note that he practiced the principle of discovering leaders through prayer:

> One of those days Jesus went out to a mountainside to pray, and spent the night praying to God. When morning came, he called his disciples to him and chose twelve of them, whom he also designated apostles.
> (Lk. 6:12-13)

Jesus not only practiced the principle of discovering leaders through prayer, He told us to do the same. Note what He told His disciples, as recorded by Matthew:

Then he said to his disciples, "The harvest is plentiful but the workers are few. Ask the Lord of the harvest, therefore, to send out workers into his harvest field."

(Mt. 9: 37-38)

In my second year of college, I was excited about spiritual reproduction. I wanted to reproduce, but I had no disciples. So I began to make it an important part of my prayer life. Every day I prayed, "Lord, give me a disciple."

Exactly two weeks later, a fellow student approached me about discipling him. The only time we were both able to meet in our dorm was late at night. The only place available was in an open area in the bathroom/shower area of our dorm. So we met every night, calling ourselves the "Bathroom Baptist Temple."

Lesson #48: The secret to discovering potential leaders is to ask God for them.

Discipling this guy was so fulfilling I asked God for another disciple. Exactly two weeks later, a guy approached us and said, "Every night for the last two weeks I have listened to you two guys while brushing my teeth. I would love to get in on what you are doing. Can I join?" So the Bathroom Baptist Temple expanded from two to three.

It was so much fun, I asked for yet another disciple and prayed each day about it. Exactly two weeks later another guy approached us. He was the roommate of the second guy. He said, "I don't know what you guys are doing every night, but my roommate is a different person. How do I join the Bathroom Baptist Temple?" So the B.B.T. went from three to four.

We were having such a good time I asked for yet *another* disciple during my prayer time. You guessed it! Exactly two weeks later, we added our fifth member. He also had seen what we were doing and wanted to be a part. At this point, we outgrew the bathroom and the dorm supervisor gave us an empty dorm room in which to meet. By the end of the semester, it was full of guys meeting several nights a week for Scripture memory, Bible study, accountability, and prayer.

This was one of the best times of my life. I had the opportunity to pour my life into other young men. We developed good friendships. All of us grew from the accountability offered in the group. Each guy said the group changed his life. The next semester our group multiplied into five groups, with each of the original members as a new leader. Through this amazing experience, I learned that the key for discovering potential leaders was persistent prayer.

God is always looking for potential leaders. Multiplying leaders is cooperating with God in *His* plan to find and mentor potential leaders into multiplying leaders. It's all about getting in on what God is already doing, and working with God in discovering potential leaders. Therefore, prayer is of the utmost importance.

Action Points:

1. Every day, ask God to send you someone to disciple and train to lead a small group.

2. Once you have an apprentice, ask God to send the apprentice someone he or she can train. Pray about this together until your apprentice has an apprentice.

[Parts of this chapter, adapted from chapter one of Dave Earley's *Turning Members into Leaders*, (Houston, TX: Touch Publications, 2003).]

Chapter 49

Four Steps for Developing New Leaders

By Dave

Kent leads a small group at our daughter church. In less than a year his group has already successfully multiplied. In an email I just received from him, he said that his "small' group wasn't small anymore … they had 30 in group the night before. Then he wrote, "I guess it's time to multiply again!"

Wow! What an exciting challenge it is to lead a healthy, growing group. But the real challenge is to fully develop the potential leaders for new groups in order to successfully multiply. Group multiplication will never happen without developing potential leaders. I like what Joel Comiskey wrote: "The principle job of the cell leader is to train the next cell leader — not just fill the house with guests."[1]

I have spent the last 30 years on a quest to learn how to mentor and multiply effective leaders. I started by studying the disciple-making ministry of Jesus. I then studied the multiplying ministry of Barnabas into the life of Paul. I also read everything I could find on disciple-making, leadership development, and small group ministry. I attended many seminars and listened to more tapes than I can count. I talked with effective pastors and Christian leaders. And, like a mad scientist, I experimented with what I learned to see how it worked. I have come to see the steps, principles, and practices Jesus used for developing effective leaders reinforced again and again in my ministry experience. I have taught these four steps for developing leaders to hundreds of pastors, Christian leaders, missionaries, and small group leaders. Here they are for you to learn and adopt.

Lesson #49: Effective small group leaders multiply their groups by intentionally training someone to lead.

Model it

Ask potential leaders to watch as you do the ministry, just as Jesus did with His disciples (Mt. 9:32-38). Let them see a highly effective small group leader in action. When Paul and Barnabas were sent out to minister, Barnabas was the leader. Barnabas was *doing* the ministry and Paul was *observing*. Note how they are listed as "Barnabas and Paul" (Acts 13:1-5).

Mentor it

Ask them do a task as you watch, assist, gently correct, and encourage as Jesus did with his disciples (Mt. 10:1). Not long into their journey, Barnabas moved over to give Paul the opportunity to lead. Note that they now were listed as "Paul and Barnabas" (Acts 13:6ff).

Motivate it

Let them do the task as you encourage from a distance, as Jesus did when he sent his disciples out two by two without him (Mt. 10:5). Similarly, when Paul and Barnabas prepared for another missionary journey, Paul was ready to go on his own (Acts 15:36-41).

Multiply it

The original disciples multiplied out to a total of 70 (Lk. 10:1), then perhaps 500 (1 Cor. 15:6). After Jesus ascended to heaven, the number of disciples multiplied to 3,000 (Acts 2:41), then 5,000 men (Acts 4:4). Then there were so many that the Bible simply says the number was multiplied (Acts 6:7).

In like fashion, Paul was soon ministering without the help of Barnabas and beginning to take others, including Silas and Timothy, through the process (Acts 15:39-41; 16:1-3). In Acts 17:14, we read where Paul left Timothy and Silas to minister in Berea on their own.

Putting the Four Steps Together

Here is an example of how this process works for training someone to facilitate a small group meeting:

Betty asks Debbie to be her apprentice. They agree to meet the night before the group each week to pray and prepare for the meeting.

Model it. Month one, Betty does all the preparation and leading, while Debbie watches. Betty is careful to explain what, why, and how she is doing things along the way.

Mentor it. Month two, Debbie prepares the icebreaker. She practices it in front of Betty. Betty makes some encouraging and helpful comments. Then Debbie leads the icebreaker in the group. Betty gives her more encouragement and helpful feedback when they get together in their weekly meeting.

Motivate it. Month three, Debbie leads the icebreaker all by herself. Occasionally, Debbie is given helpful feedback and far more encouragement.

Multiply it. Month four, Debbie shares the icebreaker with confidence and skill.

If Betty is smart, she will do basically the same thing with each piece of the meeting until Debbie can do each element confidently.

Jesus gave us a simple, yet powerful way to train and release new leaders with this four step process. I've used it many times successfully. If you will embrace it you too will produce confident and competent leaders for new small groups.

Action Points:

1. Consider the four parts of the process and the potential leaders in your group. Which parts have you done with them and what's the next step? Share this with your coach or pastor and put it into action.

2. Pray daily for your future leaders, asking God to give them confidence to lead and grow, seeing themselves as leaders.

Notes:
1. Joel Comiskey, *Leadership Explosion*, (Houston TX: TOUCH Publications, 2000), p. 40.

[This article is adapted from chapter six of the book, *Eight Habits of Effective Small Group Leaders* by Dave Earley, (Houston TX: TOUCH Publications: 2001).]

Chapter 50

Three Ways to Birth a New Group

By Dave

As a pastor, I was regularly asked to visit people in the hospital. Some visits were far more fun than others, such as the visits to the labor and delivery ward. The happiest place in any hospital is where the new fathers, aunts, uncles, and grandparents have their noses pressed against the big glass window looking proudly at the new baby!

In a similar fashion, there is nothing better for a leader than seeing one's group give birth. While there are several ineffective ways to birth new groups, there is no single "right way" to birth a group. Any form or combination of the three basic methods below will be highly effective.

Multiply: Two groups of equal size multiply from parent group

The vision of multiplication is shared. A new leader and/or leadership team develops. Relationships are formed so the team is strong. Group members are then given the option of staying with the original leaders or being a part of the new group. (Visit with each member in private to talk this through.) The goal in this multiplication strategy is to have an equal amount of members committed to each group.

Launch: A core group from parent group launches a new group

As in the first option, the vision of multiplication is shared. A new leadership team develops and relationships are formed. Group members are given the option of staying with the original leaders or being a part of the new group. However, having equal halves is not necessarily the goal. The new leaders understand that the new group will be launched without many members from the parent group.

Plant: One person from the parent group plants a new group

The planter can be either the original leader or a new leader. He or she launches a new group with new members in the church, people from the community, members of other groups who want to start a new group, or a combination of all of the above.

Suggestions for a Successful Multiplication

Talk about multiplying early and often.

Start talking about new groups forming from

day one. Describe the fact that one of the purposes of the group is to raise up leaders who will be sent out to lead new groups. At least monthly, take time to pray during your meeting about the new groups.

Keep your group informed of the plans and progress each step along the way and it will be far easier when multiplication time arrives. Remember, "people are down on what they are not up on."

> **Lesson #50: Small groups can multiply in numerous ways.**

Talk about multiplying your group in positive terms.

Do not speak of "breaking up," "splitting," or "dividing" your group. This just sounds like divorce. Instead, talk about 'birthing" new groups, "launching" new groups, "multiplying" groups, and "raising up and releasing" new leaders. Words are powerful.

Talk about multiplying in terms of the big picture.

Every new group formed lowers the number of unchurched people on the planet. New small groups equals reaching our world for Christ. Share this "big picture" view often.

Pray about the best method and the best time to multiply.

It is possible to make the right decision at the wrong time. Maybe the group is ready to multiply, but the new leader(s) are not. Or maybe the new leader(s) are ready, but the group is not. Or maybe it is a poor season to launch (Summer is usually not a good season to launch). Pray about the best timing for your multiplication with your group and your coach or pastor.

Set a date for multiplication.

Setting a date for multiplying your group is essential in achieving the dream of multiplying your group according to Joel Comiskey's survey of 700 multiplying small group leaders from around the world:

> Cell leaders who know their goal — when their groups will give birth — consistently multiply their groups more often than leaders who don't know. In fact, if a cell leader fails to set goals the cell members can clearly remember, he has about a 50-50 chance of multiplying his cell. But if the leader sets goals, the chance of multiplying increases to three of four.[1]

Celebrate the new birth.

When your small group is ready to give birth, throw a party and invite your friends and your coach. Ask your small groups pastor to preside over a special time of prayer, sending out the new group(s) and leader(s). This is a great opportunity to recast the vision for multiplying. Some churches make this a part of their worship celebration to make a visual statement of their priorities and vision. (If your church doesn't do this today, ask your pastor if your group's multiplication could be celebrated by praying over the new group during an upcoming worship service.)

There are many ways to multiply a group when you consider the combinations of the three ways described in this chapter. The goal of multiplication is to insure the new group and the existing groups remain strong with healthy members and competent leaders. Bathe your multiplication in prayer, talk through everything with the members and leaders involved, and move forward in confidence. God is on your side when you multiply leaders and groups!

Action Points:

1. Review the three basic multiplication strategies and discuss each one with your apprentice. Ask him or her which one provides the greatest level of excitement.

2. Then, pray together and ask God to work it all out and give you both wisdom as to how to proceed and when to multiply your group.

Notes:
1. Joel Comiskey, *Home Group Cell Explosion,* (Houston, TX, TOUCH Publications, 1998), p. 47.

Chapter 51

The Roles and Responsibilities of a P.A.C.E.-Setting Apprentice

By Dave

Excited small group leaders typically ask questions like, "What should I expect from an apprentice?" or, "What's a reasonable amount of responsibility on their part?" or, "What type of commitment should I ask them to make?"

When I am working with an apprentice who is new to group leadership, I ask for four basic commitments.

Setting the P.A.C.E.

Pray. My apprentices are expected to pray for group members daily.

I usually give the apprentice 4-10 names of group members they are to pray for each day. This creates a heart for the people within the new leader. It also increases God's work in the group member's lives and the quality and quantity of prayer in the group. It also frees me (the mentoring leader) from praying for too many people. As a leader, I generally only pray daily for my apprentices and weekly for each member of my group.

Availability. My apprentices are expected to be available to group members between meetings.

I have a strong personality as a leader. In order to multiply, I must wean group members from me as quickly as possible. I also want to build the bridge between my apprentice and group members as quickly as possible. Therefore, I ask my apprentices to give their phone numbers to the group members they are praying for each day. I expect my apprentices to be the first ones to visit those people if they have a need.

Contact. My apprentices are expected to contact group members weekly.

Every week I expect my apprentices to call each of the group members for whom they are praying. This is what I've termed a "five-minute phone call." This call helps the group member feel like someone cares for them. It also builds the relationships that pave the way for the eventual multiplication of the group. It further frees me (the leader) from needing to call all the group members every week. When my apprentices are calling members, I can focus on reaching new people.

During the call, the apprentice may ask the group members such things as:

"How are you doing?"

"What can I pray for you about?"

"What did you like about the group last night?"

"Have you ever thought about becoming an apprentice?"

"What week would you like to bring refreshments for the group?"

"We have been praying for your friend at work. Did she say if she was coming to church this week or not?"

Lesson #51: Your members will follow your apprentices into a new group if they will pray, remain available, contact the members, and be a positive example.

They may also say things such as:

"I want you to know that I really appreciated what you shared last week in our group."

"I want to remind you to put our group's party on your calendar."

"When I pray about those who could become apprentices when our group multiplies, your name keeps coming to mind."

Example. My apprentices are expected to be positive examples for the members of the group.

When you start talking about being an example, some people become intimidated. So, I speak of being a positive example of a *progressing* Christian, not a *perfect* Christian. How you define a progressive Christian will change from setting to setting. In the context of small group leadership, I expect my apprentices to set an example for the other members of the group with daily Bible reading and prayer, faithful church attendance, and reading the book I have given them on small group leadership.

P.A.C.E.+M

After an apprentice has been fulfilling the four commitments for a few months, I generally add the fifth commitment. At this point the commitment shifts from P.A.C.E. to P.A.C.E.M. (another corny pun, but memorable ... therefore, it works).

<u>M</u>entor. My apprentices are expected to mentor the person who will become their apprentice when they launch the new group.

Multiplication rarely "just happens." It is always the result of intentional decisions and commitments. In order to instill multiplication into the DNA of your group, help your apprentice find a future leader while they are still in your group. This will give them vision for the future group and help them start strong.

The wise small group leader doesn't simultaneously require all five commitments of brand new apprentices. First, the apprentice is asked to pray daily for members. After a few weeks of doing this, their level of availability between meetings will naturally increase as they adopt God's heart for people. When this happens, calling the members is enjoyable and deep relationships form. Throughout this process, a good leader encourages his or her apprentices to spend quality time with God in the Word and to be faithful to the church in tithing and attendance. Finally, helping them do the same thing by mentoring another member in these commitments will give them everything they need to become a life-long, disciple-making small group leader.

Action Points:

1. Re-read this chapter aloud to your apprentice(s) and ask which of the commitments they want to work on with your encouragement.

2. Spend quality time with your apprentices each week outside of the meeting. Prepare for the next meeting, pray for them, and enjoy one another's company doing something fun together such as going to a ball game, having dinner together, or kicking back and watching a movie together with your families.

[Parts of this chapter are adapted from chapter six of Dave Earley's, *Turning Members into Leaders*, (Houston, TX: TOUCH Publications, 2003).]

Chapter 52

How to Keep From Losing Heart in Ministry

By Dave

Many small group leaders begin their ministry highly motivated and full of optimism and energy. But within a few years, they lose heart. These leaders find themselves merely going through the motions or they give up on leadership all together and close their group.

This is understandable. The moment you step up to lead, you place a target on your back. You attract a greater level of attention from the enemy than ever before. Beyond that, a small group is a refuge for needy people. It can be a place of extreme fatigue and endless frustration for those who attempt to minister to people's needs. Life is messy, people have problems, and ministry is often chaotic and frustrating. Calling people to a life of discipleship can also be disappointing. Even Jesus had dropouts and disappointments.

Very few small group leaders face the level of temptation to quit that the apostle Paul dealt with. How did he keep from losing heart in the ministry despite such intense difficulties? He lived with an eternal perspective.

In 2 Corinthians 4, Paul pulled back the veil to

give us a look into his view of ministry. He reveals several essentials for maintaining the right perspective.

Be grateful

"Therefore, since through God's mercy we have this ministry, we do not lose heart" (1 Corinthians 4:1, The Message). We become discouraged and want to quit when we feel that we are entitled to more or better. Don't forget, being allowed to minister to others is a gift to be appreciated, not a right to be demanded. We only minister because God is merciful. He allows messed up, "ex-sinners" like you and me to have the privilege and honor of serving Him by ministering to His people.

Keep it real

"We refuse to wear masks and play games. We don't maneuver and manipulate behind the scenes. And we don't twist God's Word to suit ourselves. Rather, we keep everything we do and say out in the open, the whole truth on display, so that those who want to can see and judge for themselves in the presence of God" (2 Corinthians 4:2, The Message).

The *persona* is the mask that was worn in an ancient Greek tragedy. Psychologists speak of the persona as that psychological mask used to cover our true inner feelings when we relate to others. It takes a great deal of energy to

> **Lesson #52:**
> **The way to battle discouragement is to maintain the right perspective.**

keep the persona polished and clean. Wearing one can make you appear artificial or fake. Therefore, invest your time and effort being your best self, as opposed to trying to be someone you are not.

Reflect Christ, not self

"*Remember, our Message is not about ourselves; we're proclaiming Jesus Christ, the Master. All we are is messengers, errand runners from Jesus for you ... If you only look at us, you might well miss the brightness. We carry this precious Message around in the unadorned clay pots of our ordinary lives. That's to prevent anyone from confusing God's incomparable power with us. As it is, there's not much chance of that. You know for yourselves that we're not much to look at*" (2 Corinthians 4:5-7, The Message).

I find the most energy in ministry comes when I take God very seriously and don't take myself too seriously. You will last in ministry when you learn to accept your shortcomings, admit your mistakes, and laugh at yourself as you place the focus on Christ.

Stay positive

"*We've been surrounded and battered by troubles, but we're not demoralized; we're not sure what to do, but we know that God knows what to do; we've been spiritually terrorized, but God hasn't left our side; we've been thrown down, but we haven't broken. What they did to Jesus, they do to us — trial and tor-ture, mockery and murder; what Jesus did among them, he does in us — he lives! Our lives are at con-*

stant risk for Jesus' sake, which makes Jesus' life all the more evident in us. While we're going through the worst, you're getting in on the best! ... Every detail works to your advantage and to God's glory: more and more grace, more and more people, more and more praise!" (2 Corinthians 4:8-15, The Message).

Paul was gifted at seeing the spiritual, the eternal, and the positive in every circumstance. His suffering actually brought him joy because he was able to see how God was using it to multiply his ministry. Therefore, he did not let any setback leave him discouraged.

Focus on the Invisible Glory of Eternity

"So we're not giving up. How could we! Even though on the outside it often looks like things are falling apart on us, on the inside, where God is making new life, not a day goes by without his unfolding grace. These hard times are small potatoes compared to the coming good times, the lavish celebration prepared for us. There's far more here than meets the eye. The things we see now are here today, gone tomorrow. But the things we can't see now will last forever" (2 Corinthians 4:16-18, The Message).

Eternity is a very long time. As you serve the Lord as a small group leader, you are making investments that will last forever. Therefore, don't give up! One day, it will be worth it all when you see how you have built the kingdom of God.

Action Points:

1. Open your Bible and underline the verses quoted in this chapter and put today's date in the margin. When you read these verses in the future, remember the day you underlined them and thank the Lord for the opportunity to serve and represent Him among His people.

2. Pray for the other small group leaders in your church by name this week, asking God to encourage them and prevent them from becoming battle weary. When you see them at leadership meetings or during services, tell them you prayed for them ... which is always encouraging.

Other Excellent Resources by Dave Earley

8 HABITS OF EFFECTIVE SMALL GROUP LEADERS
by Dave Earley

Dave Earley has identified eight habits of effective small group leaders: Dream; Pray; Invite; Contact; Prepare; Mentor; Fellowship and Grow. When your leaders adopt and practice these habits, your groups will undoubtedly multiply. If you like what you've read in this pocket book, you'll love the expanded help you'll find in the original book.

TURNING MEMBERS INTO LEADERS
by Dave Earley

The best way to raise up new small group leaders is not to ask them to be leaders until they've been covertly trained and prepared for the role. This excellent resource explains how to turn members into leaders who will say "Yes!" to leadership when you pop the question. If your small group ministry needs more leaders, this book is a must-read for every small group leader and coach!

These titles can be purchased with substantial discounts off the retail price through the publisher, TOUCH® Publications, Houston, Texas.

1-800-735-5865 • www.touchusa.org